FACTS AT YOUR FINGERTIPS

INTRODUCING PHYSICS
MAGNETISM

CONTENTS

Published by Brown Bear Books Limited

4877 N. Circulo Bujia
Tucson, AZ 85718
USA
and
First Floor
9-17 St. Albans Place
London N1 0NX
UK
www.brownreference.com

© 2010 The Brown Reference Group Ltd

Library of Congress Cataloging-in-Publication Data

Magnetism / edited by Graham Bateman.
     p. cm. – (Facts at your fingertips)
  Includes index.
  ISBN 978-1-936333-08-0 (library binding)
  1. Magnetism–Juvenile literature. 2. Magnets–Juvenile literature. I.
Bateman, Graham. II. Title. III. Series.

QC753.7.M34 2010
538–dc22

2010015490

ISBN-13 978-1-936333-08-0

Editorial Director: Lindsey Lowe
Project Director: Graham Bateman
Design Manager: David Poole
Designer: Steve McCurdy
Text Editors: Peter Lewis, Briony Ryles
Indexer: David Bennett
Children's Publisher: Anne O'Daly
Production Director: Alastair Gourlay

Printed in the United States of America

Picture Credits
Abbreviations: SS=Shutterstock; c=center; t=top; l=left; r=right.
Cover Images
Front: SS: Alex Back: SS: Roman Sigaev
1 SS: Jozsef Szasz-Fabian; 3 Photos.com; 4 Photos.com; 7 SS: Awe
Inspiring Images; 11 Photos.com; 12-13 NASA/ESA, John Clarke;
15 SS: Terry Alexander; 18-19 SS: Siloto; 20 SS: Gonul Kokal; 22-23
SS: James Stedl; 24-25 Wikimedia Commons: Rama; 27 Wikimedia
Commons: Daniel Schwen; 28 SS: Jiri Vaclavek; 29 Wikimedia
Commons; 31 Photos.com; 32 Photos.com; 34-35 SS: Jozsef Szasz-
Fabian; 38-39 SS: Marek Slusarczyk; 41l SS: Tim Arbaek; 41r SS:
Brandon Blinkenberg; 42-43 Wikimedia Commons; Siemens

Pressebild; 44 SS: Dragon Fang; 46-47 SS: Natalia Bratslavsky;
48-49 SS: Richard Thornton; 49 SS: PHB.cz (Richard Semik); 50-
51 SS: Anton Foltin; 52-53 Photos.com; 55 SS: Gyukli Gyula; 56-
57 Photos.com; 58 SS: David Gaylor.

Artwork © The Brown Reference Group Ltd

*The Brown Reference Group Ltd has made every effort to trace
copyright holders of the pictures used in this book. Anyone having
claims to ownership not identified above is invited to contact The
Brown Reference Group Ltd.*

Facts at your Fingertips—Introducing Physics describes the processes and practical implications fundamental to the study of physics. People have long been fascinated by the way magnets attract pieces of iron, but it has taken modern physics to explain how they do it. In this volume, we describe the properties of magnets and their uses. The intimate connection between electricity and magnetism that is key to modern life is explored—electric currents generate magnetic fields, and magnetic fields, when they alter, can drive electric currents. Electromagnets are used in many devices from the electric bell to pollution-free electric cars. Ultimately the generation of much of our electricity relies on generators in which powerful magnets are the key. Finally we describe how another form of electricity generation and storage is achieved through various types of batteries.

Numerous explanatory diagrams and informative photographs, detailed features on related aspects of the topics covered and the main scientists involved in the advancement of physics, and definitions of key "Science Words," all enhance the coverage. "Try This" features outline experiments that can be undertaken as a first step to practical investigations.

MAGNETIC MATERIALS

A magnetic rock called lodestone has a power that seemed magical to early people. It can point to the north and guide a traveler even when all landmarks are hidden by night or in bad weather. Early explorers used this "magic" on sea voyages.

Among the earth's many types of rock is a very unusual one, first recognized as early as 2700 B.C. by Chinese scholars. This rock, called lodestone (or magnetite, to give it its modern name), contains iron. It attracts other metals, and pieces of it will either attract or repel each other depending on how they are oriented.

Lodestone demonstrates another amazing property when it is set up so that it can turn freely. It will then turn until it is pointing roughly north-south. This magnetic "compass" may have been used by navigators as early as the 3rd century A.D. in China. Certainly it was in widespread use by European sailors in the 12th century.

A magnetic needle enabled this portable sundial to be aligned north-south to take a correct reading. The instrument doubled as a magnetic compass.

MAGNETIC DOMAINS

Tiny areas in a piece of iron, called domains, are like individual magnets. Applying a magnetic field lines up these magnets. The metal is said to be saturated when all the domains have their magnetism lined up.

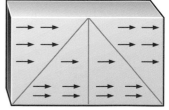

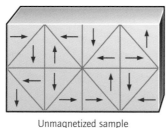

Unmagnetized sample

Magnetic field applied

Saturated sample

North

SCIENCE WORDS

- **Atom:** The smallest part of a chemical element that can exist on its own. It has a central nucleus, surrounded by electrons.
- **Domain:** A small region in a magnetic material in which the magnetic fields of individual atoms all point in the same direction, making the domain into a single small magnet. In the unmagnetized material, fields of different domains point in different directions, canceling one another out.
- **Lodestone:** A naturally magnetic iron ore, formerly used to make magnetic compasses. It is one of only two minerals that is naturally magnetic; the other, pyrrhotite, has only weak magnetism.

Supplies of lodestone were limited. But it was possible to use a piece of lodestone to make a large number of magnetic needles for use in compasses. By stroking an iron needle with the lodestone many times, always in the same direction, the iron became magnetized.

In the 20th century, this effect was explained by the French physicist Pierre-Ernest Weiss (1865–1940). Individual atoms of iron and other elements present in a piece of metal are like miniature magnets. The metal is divided into regions called domains in which all the atoms line up. The magnetism of the atoms adds together, making each domain into a tiny magnet. But the atoms in different domains point in different directions, so that overall the piece of metal does not behave like a magnet. Repeated stroking with a piece of lodestone causes the atoms to turn. Eventually they all point in the same direction, and their magnetism adds up to make the whole piece of metal a strong magnet. When all the atoms are lined up and the magnetism cannot become any greater, the piece of metal is said to be saturated.

TRY THIS

How much pull?

Magnets vary in strength, usually depending on how large they are. One way to measure the strength of a magnet is to see how much it will lift up.

What to do

Using masking tape, tape down a bar magnet near the edge of a table, with one end sticking out over the edge. Add paper clips to the end, building up a chain of clips hanging down. What is the maximum number of clips the magnet will hold up? Repeat the procedure, this time using a horseshoe magnet. How many clips will this magnet hold up?

The first clip is held by magnetism. The clip is made of steel, which is a magnetic material. When it is in contact with the magnet, this clip also becomes a magnet. The new paper-clip magnet holds up the second clip. That also becomes a magnet, and so on, all along the chain of paper clips. The number of clips held up is a measure of the strength of the magnet. Generally, a horseshoe magnet is stronger than a bar magnet of the same overall length.

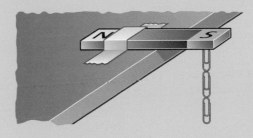

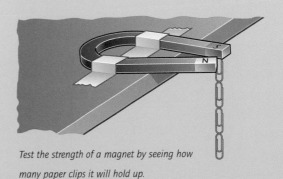

Test the strength of a magnet by seeing how many paper clips it will hold up.

MAGNETIC POLES AND FIELDS

Surrounding a magnet and extending into nearby space is a "sphere of influence" called a magnetic field. How another magnet is affected by the first magnet depends both on this magnetic field and on the second magnet's own properties.

A piece of lodestone or other magnet will attract small metal objects to itself. The way they arrange themselves around the magnet reveals to us important facts about magnetism. Iron filings—tiny metal grains produced when a block of iron is filed or machined—show this especially clearly. They cluster around the two ends of a bar magnet, but not toward its middle. If the magnet is in the shape of a horseshoe, the filings cluster at the ends of the two "legs," but not around

Iron filings scattered around the poles of a bar magnet reveal the magnetic field around them. Each filing orients itself in the direction of the field at its location, and together they trace a dramatic picture of the whole magnetic field.

its middle. Every magnet has these two "attractive ends," called its poles.

One of the poles of a magnet is attracted to the north and the other to the south. This is the reason why a compass needle swings until it is pointing north–south. The north-seeking pole is called the magnet's north, or N, pole; the south-seeking pole is the south, or S, pole.

Attraction of opposites

When the two north poles of a magnet are brought close to each other, they can be felt to repel each other. The closer together they are, the harder is the

---

ONE OR TWO POLES

These fields are produced by one or two magnetic poles. Such poles always occur in linked pairs; but if they are widely separated, they can be regarded as single poles.

PLOTTING THE FIELD

Trails of dots marking successive positions of the head and tail of the compass needle trace out field lines.

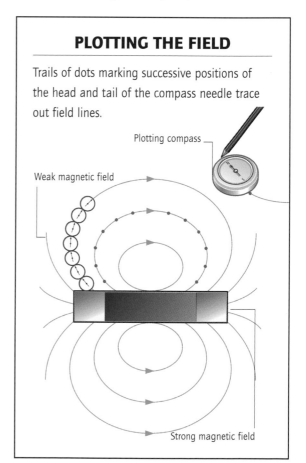

Plotting compass

Weak magnetic field

Strong magnetic field

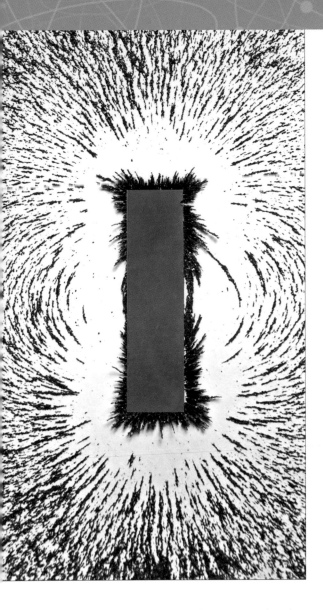

To map the field, put the magnet on a piece of paper and place the compass anywhere on the paper. Mark the two ends of the needle with pencil dots. Then move the compass until the tail of the needle is just over the dot that marks the previous position of the head of the needle. Mark the new position of the head of the needle, and again move the compass until the tail of the needle is at that position. Continue repeating this process.

The result is a chain of dots that can be joined up smoothly to make a curved line. At every point along this line the direction of the line is the direction of the compass at that point, which is the direction of the force that would be experienced by any magnetic object at that point. The curved line is called a line of force or a field line. The region in which magnetic forces are experienced is the magnetic field. Field lines indicate the north–south direction.

Picturing the field

The magnetic field can also be made visible in a striking way with the aid of iron filings. If a sheet of paper is placed over a magnet and iron filings are shaken over the paper, many cluster directly over the

mutual push. The same happens if the two south poles are brought close to each other. But when a north pole is brought close to a south pole, a force of attraction can be felt. Again, the force is stronger the closer the poles are to each other.

The field can be "mapped" with the aid of a small compass. If it is brought close to a magnet, the needle of the compass points toward or away from the nearest pole of the magnet. If the nearest pole is a south pole, the north-seeking end of the needle points toward it. If the compass is moved toward the other end of the magnet, the effect of the north pole gradually increases, and the needle turns until its south-seeking end points toward the north pole.

FORCES BETWEEN MAGNETS

Two bar magnets suspended on strings will push each other apart or pull each other together depending on whether like poles (two N or two S) or unlike poles (N and S) are closest to each other.

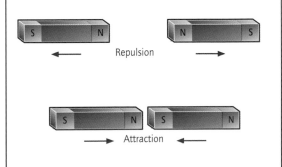

Repulsion

Attraction

TRY THIS

Field of force

The region around a magnet in which it attracts metal objects is called its magnetic field. The field is invisible, yet it can be shown. This project shows you how to reveal the existence of a magnetic field and discover its shape.

What to do

Put some iron filings in a cup and sprinkle them thinly onto a piece of writing paper. Carefully slide the paper into a clear plastic pocket, and tape closed the open edge of the pocket (this keeps the filings from spilling and possibly sticking to the magnet). Put the magnet on a table, and place the pocket on top of it. The filings will arrange themselves in a pattern that corresponds to the magnetic field of the magnet. Repeat the procedure with another shape of magnet if you have one. You can even use the same method to find the shape of the magnetic field between two magnets. The iron filings line themselves up along the lines of force that make up the magnetic field. The field is strongest near the poles (ends) of the magnet, which is why the filings concentrate at these points. If you use two magnets, you can see how their magnetic fields combine.

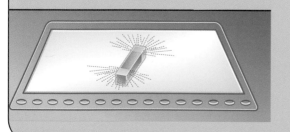

The iron filings inside the plastic pocket will reveal the magnetic field.

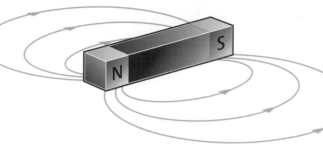

Field lines, or lines of force, are imaginary lines showing the force that the magnet would exert on an imaginary north magnetic pole. At each point the direction of the field line shows the direction of the force.

poles. But some lie scattered over the rest of the area around the magnet and arrange themselves in curved lines. The lines run from one pole to the other. They are formed as each individual grain lines up in a certain direction. Each grain acts like a tiny magnetic compass and points in a definite direction. Together they give a vivid picture of the form of the field, and even of its strength, for the lines crowd together near poles, where the field is strongest. The more the field lines spread out, the weaker the field is.

The direction of the field at a point is defined as the direction of the force that would be experienced by the north pole of another magnet at that point. According to this definition, the field lines run outside the magnet from its north pole toward its south pole. Entering the magnet near the south pole, they return toward the north pole, each forming a closed loop. Field lines do not normally meet or cross one another.

Poles apart

Every magnet has two opposite poles: no isolated pole is known to exist. (Physicists have made searches for subatomic particles that are single magnetic poles, but such "monopoles" have never been discovered.) This makes working out the laws of the magnetic field difficult. It is easier to see what is happening with a very long bar magnet, with the poles far apart. The magnetic effects of each pole can then be studied while the influence of the other one is ignored.

The strength of the magnetic field produced by a single pole can be measured at each point in space by measuring the force on another magnetic pole placed there. It is found that the strength of the field falls to one-fourth when the distance is doubled, to one-ninth when it is tripled, to one-sixteenth when it is increased fourfold, and so on. That is to say, the field strength is inversely proportional to the square of the distance. (Many other physical quantities also fall off in strength proportional to the square of the distance, including the strength of gravity and of electrical fields, and the brightness of light.)

The strength of the magnetic field at a given point depends not only on how far from the magnet that point is, but also on the strength of the magnet itself. A particular piece of iron, for example, can be more or less strongly magnetized. (The word "magnetic" describes a material that can be made into a magnet whether or not it is a magnet now. The word "magnetized" refers to a magnetic material that actually is a magnet.) Magnetic materials include iron, cobalt, and nickel, and alloys such as steel. Scientists have also created nonmetallic materials called ferrites that can be made into powerful magnets.

SCIENCE WORDS

- **Bar magnet:** A permanent magnet that is bar-shaped, having a magnetic pole at each end.
- **Field:** The pattern of magnetic, electric, gravitational, or other influence around an object. See also Line of force.
- **Line of force:** An imaginary line whose direction at any point in a field shows the direction of the field at that point.
- **Pole:** One of the two regions of a magnet where the strength of the field is greatest. Lines of force diverge (radiate out) from one pole and converge on the other.

A FORCE BETWEEN POLES

Two north poles repel each other, as do two south poles. A north and a south pole attract each other. The force between two magnetic poles is proportional to M_1 and M_2, the strengths of the magnets, and inversely proportional to d^2, the square of the distance between them.

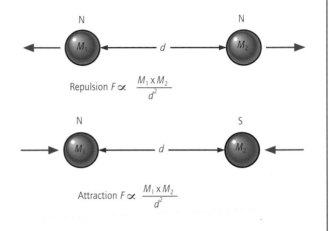

Repulsion $F \propto \dfrac{M_1 \times M_2}{d^2}$

Attraction $F \propto \dfrac{M_1 \times M_2}{d^2}$

FIELDS BETWEEN MAGNETS

When two bar magnets are brought near each other, the shapes of the field lines between them depend on which poles are involved.

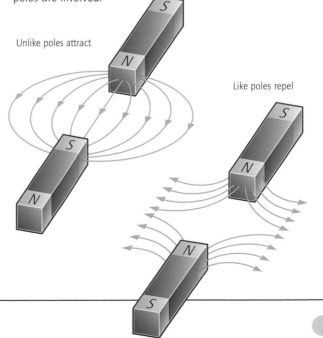

Unlike poles attract

Like poles repel

EARTH'S MAGNETISM

We live on a giant magnet. The turning of the Earth's core generates our planet's magnetic field, which not only influences compasses, but reaches far into space. It changes slowly with time, and the record of these changes is written in the rocks, revealing the planet's geological history billions of years into the past.

The Earth's magnetic field is like that of a huge bar magnet deep within the planet and aligned quite closely with the Earth's axis of rotation. The poles of this imaginary magnet lie beneath two opposite points on the Earth's surface, close to the geographical poles, where the field lines are vertical. The points on the surface are called the Earth's north and south magnetic poles. The magnetic equator is the imaginary line around the Earth, halfway between the magnetic poles, where the field lines are horizontal.

Shifting, multicolored auroras are often seen in the sky in polar regions. They are caused by electrically charged particles, mostly from the Sun, being funneled by the Earth's magnetic field down from space toward the magnetic poles.

THE EARTH AS A MAGNET

The lines of force of the Earth's magnetic field can be traced just as they can for a small magnet. The field has the same shape as the magnetic field of a bar magnet. The north magnetic pole lies about 800 miles (1,300 km) from the geographical north pole. The south magnetic pole is about twice as far as this from the geographical south pole.

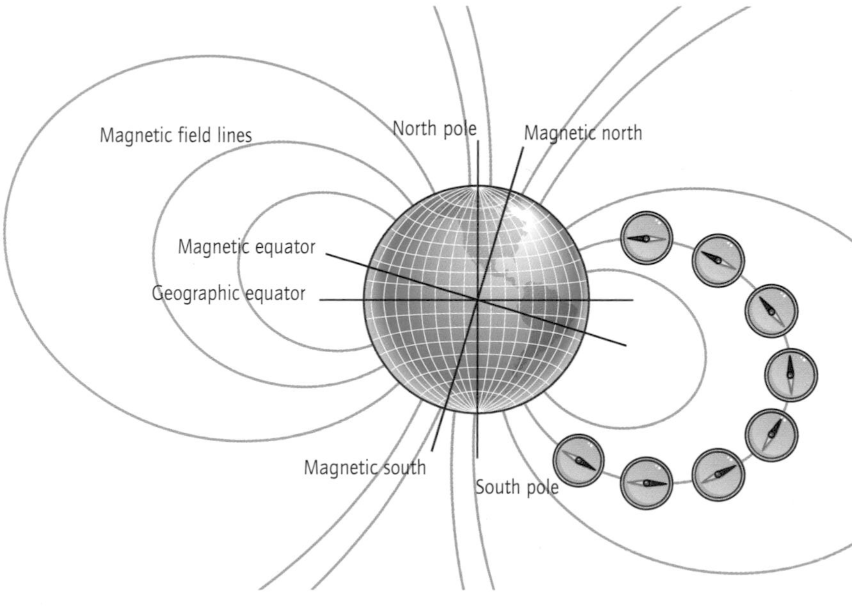

Magnetic field lines

North pole

Magnetic north

Magnetic equator

Geographic equator

Magnetic south

South pole

ANGLE OF DIP

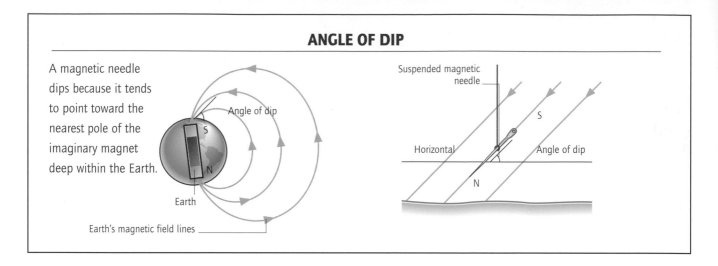

A magnetic needle dips because it tends to point toward the nearest pole of the imaginary magnet deep within the Earth.

Angle of dip

S

N

Earth

Earth's magnetic field lines

Suspended magnetic needle

S

Horizontal

Angle of dip

N

Because a magnetic compass points to the magnetic poles, it does not in general point to true north or true south. The angle between true north and "magnetic north" is called variation. The direction of magnetic north is shown on some maps. Variation changes with time because the positions of the poles change: they wander by about 12 miles (20 km) per year.

Animal navigators

Many types of animal rely, at least partly, on the Earth's magnetism to guide them. Some birds migrate from one continent to another at the beginning of summer and winter. They get their sense of direction largely from the position of the Sun or stars; but when the skies are cloudy and they cannot do that, their sense of the Earth's magnetism guides them. Water-dwelling organisms that are sensitive to the Earth's magnetic field include some bacteria, whales, dolphins, sharks, and sea turtles.

The magnetosphere

The Earth's magnetic field extends into space. Electrically charged particles that constantly flow outward from the Sun are called the solar wind. They are trapped by the Earth's magnetic field and form two thick belts of charged particles, known as the Van Allen belts.

The Earth's magnetosphere is the volume of space in which the Earth's magnetic field is stronger than that of the Sun. The solar wind squeezes the magnetosphere, so that it is 40,000 miles (64,000 km) above the surface on the sunward side of the Earth,

SCIENCE WORDS

- **Magnetosphere:** The region around the Earth or other celestial body, such as Jupiter, in which its magnetic field is stronger than the field in surrounding space.
- **Solar wind:** The stream of charged particles ejected from the Sun's upper atmosphere.
- **Van Allen belts:** Another name for the Earth's radiation belts.

but stretches into a tail, over 600,000 miles (1 million km) long, on the side away from the Sun. Some other planets, in particular Jupiter, possess magnetic fields and magnetospheres. The Sun's magnetic field is very powerful and dominates a region of space, called the heliosphere, extending beyond the distant planet Pluto.

Restless Earth

Although lodestone is the only strongly magnetized rock, many other types of rock were weakly magnetized when they were formed. The direction of their magnetic field was the same as that of the Earth at that time, but since then the rocks have moved. By patient detective work it is possible to reconstruct how the rocks have moved since their formation. This work shows that the continents have drifted over the surface of the Earth ever since a single supercontinent called Pangaea broke up about 180 million years ago.

Generator in the Earth

Electric currents in the Earth's molten outer core generate its magnetic field. In addition to the slow changes in direction of the field that cause "polar

Just like the Aurora borealis (North) and Aurora australis (South) on Earth, Jupiter's poles attract charged particles from the Sun. Seen here is the aurora around the planet's north pole, photographed by NASA's Hubble Space Telescope.

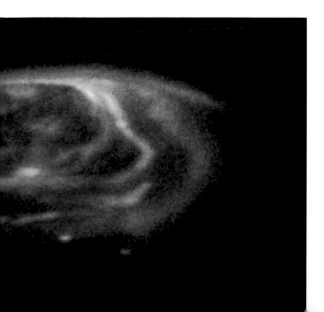

TRY THIS

Create a compass

A compass consists of a magnetized needle that is free to rotate and point in any direction. But in the Earth's magnetic field one end of the needle always points toward north. In this project, you will make a simple floating compass.

What to do

Fill a shallow bowl three-fourths full of water. Tape a sewing needle across a slice of cork or Styrofoam. Using one end of a magnet, stroke the needle 20 or 30 times along its length, always going in the same direction. Float the cork or foam with its needle in the center of the water. After a while the needle will settle down. It will point north-south, just like a real compass.

The magnetized needle lines up with the direction of the Earth's magnetic field. Because this direction is north-south, the needle also points north-south. You can deflect the needle from its north-south alignment by bringing a magnet near it. The needle would rather line up with the strong field of the magnet than with the weak field of the Earth.

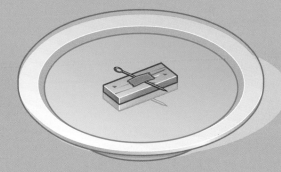

The needle on your homemade compass will settle pointing north-south.

wandering," every few hundred thousand years the field dies down to zero and then increases in strength again, now pointing in the opposite direction. The record of these field reversals is written in the magnetism of the rocks.

Compasses are the oldest science tools that make use of a magnetic field—the Earth's magnetic field. The Earth behaves as if it had a giant bar magnet along its axis between the north and south poles. The field curves around from one pole to the other.

In a magnetic compass, the pointer (called the needle) is itself a small magnet, pivoted at its center so that it can swing from side to side. When it points to the north, it is in fact indicating the direction of the Earth's magnetic field.

Magnetometer

A compass is not the only scientific instrument that uses magnets. A device called a tangent galvanometer detects electric currents by using a small pivoted magnet. Fairly similar in this respect is a magnetometer, which, as its name suggests, is an instrument for measuring the strength of a magnetic field.

The magnetometer consists of a small pivoted magnet attached at right angles to a long, nonmagnetic pointer. It is turned until the magnet lines up with the Earth's magnetic field, and the pointer indicates zero (illustration (a), left). When another magnetic field, such as that of a bar magnet, is nearby, one end of the magnet is attracted to it (because opposite magnetic poles, a north and a south, attract each other). This makes the pointer move around the scale (illustration (b), left). The angle indicated by the pointer is a measure of the strength of the external field (the actual field strength is proportional to the tangent of the indicated angle).

Just as opposite magnetic poles attract each other, similar ones—two north poles or two south poles—repel each other. This effect is put to good use in a maglev train (see page 53). Maglev is short for "magnetic levitation" (lifting); electromagnets with one polarity inside the train lift the vehicle clear of rails that have the opposite polarity. Electromagnetic effects like this are used in a wide range of devices, including electric bells, relays, loudspeakers, generators, and electric motors.

Magnetic detectors

The presence of nearby metal objects can alter a magnetic field. That is what makes metal detectors work—you may have seen them in airports or stores. The apparatus consists of a tall archway the size of a door. Large coils of wire in the sides of the arch carry an electric current, which creates a magnetic field. Anyone who walks through the arch carrying a metal

---

MAGNETOMETER

A magnetometer consists of a small pivoted magnet attached at right angles to a long pointer that indicates the direction of the magnetic field (a) of the Earth and (b) of a nearby magnet.

A metal detector works by creating a magnetic field and responding to changes in the field caused by the presence of metallic objects. Using such devices, people can sometimes unearth buried treasure.

object, such as a handgun, will disturb the magnetic field. The change in the field is detected and causes an alarm to sound. A bunch of keys or a metal watchband will also set off the alarm, which is why people are asked to remove such objects before they walk through the detector.

People searching for buried objects use a different type of metal detector. It consists of a coil of wire carrying an electric current mounted inside a disk at the end of a long handle. Batteries in the handle supply the electricity. The coil produces a magnetic field that is distorted by any metal objects in the ground. A microchip in the handle detects the tiny changes in current produced by the field distortion and causes the detector to make a buzzing or bleeping sound. Scientific versions of the instrument give an audible warning via earphones, as in the picture on the left.

More sensitive magnetometers are used in prospecting for underground minerals. To cover a large area quickly, the instrument is mounted in an aerodynamic "torpedo" and towed behind a light airplane or helicopter. It works by detecting distortions in the Earth's magnetic field (which is usually fairly regular) caused by mineral deposits. Minerals nearer the surface have a greater effect than those buried deep underground. The data from the magnetometer passes along the cable to an onboard computer in the towing aircraft.

SCIENCE WORDS

- **Maglev:** Abbreviation for "magnetic levitation", the technology for keeping vehicles such as trains a few centimeters above the track on which they run by means of mutually repelling magnetic fields, to overcome friction.

MAKING MAGNETS

Magnets were precious objects in societies that relied on them for navigation. Practical people learned methods of making magnets from iron and steel. Nowadays, we have effective ways of making the very strong magnets that various devices rely on.

It was probably in ancient times when people first discovered that hammering an iron bar while it is aligned north–south magnetizes it. If the iron is made red-hot and allowed to cool while being hammered, it gets even more strongly magnetized.

Stroking a piece of iron with a magnet also magnetizes it. Sailors used to take a piece of lodestone on voyages so that they could "refresh" their compass

HOW TO MAKE A MAGNET

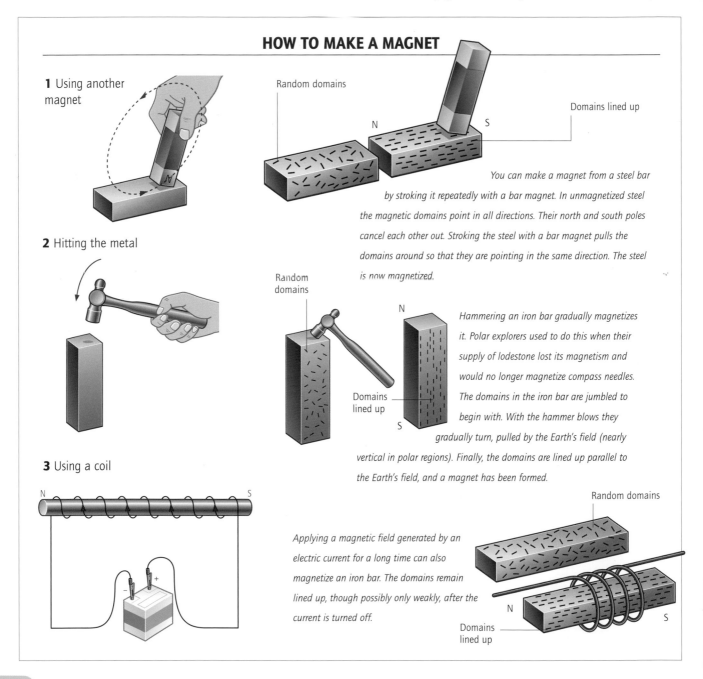

1 Using another magnet

Random domains

N   S

Domains lined up

You can make a magnet from a steel bar by stroking it repeatedly with a bar magnet. In unmagnetized steel the magnetic domains point in all directions. Their north and south poles cancel each other out. Stroking the steel with a bar magnet pulls the domains around so that they are pointing in the same direction. The steel is now magnetized.

2 Hitting the metal

Random domains

N

Domains lined up

S

Hammering an iron bar gradually magnetizes it. Polar explorers used to do this when their supply of lodestone lost its magnetism and would no longer magnetize compass needles. The domains in the iron bar are jumbled to begin with. With the hammer blows they gradually turn, pulled by the Earth's field (nearly vertical in polar regions). Finally, the domains are lined up parallel to the Earth's field, and a magnet has been formed.

3 Using a coil

N   S

Applying a magnetic field generated by an electric current for a long time can also magnetize an iron bar. The domains remain lined up, though possibly only weakly, after the current is turned off.

Random domains

N   S

Domains lined up

needles, or magnetize new ones, whenever it was necessary. Hammering an iron bar could provide a substitute for the lodestone (see the illustrations on page 16).

These methods of magnetizing the metal depend on the fact that a piece of unmagnetized iron or steel is made up of countless tiny magnets—the domains, or regions where atoms are all aligned (see pages 4–5). Because they are pointing in all directions, these domains cancel one another out, and the metal has no overall magnetization. To turn the metal into a magnet, the atoms in all the domains have to be rotated so that they all point the same way.

A very strong magnetic field can do this. A coil of wire carrying an electric current can provide such a field (see pages 24–27). The moderate field of another magnet that is made to stroke the piece of metal repeatedly can also magnetize the metal. If the north pole of the magnet makes contact with the metal being magnetized, it will pull the south poles of the atomic magnets toward itself. A south pole will develop at the end of the metal where the magnet breaks contact.

The Earth's magnetic field is strong enough to align the atoms and magnetize the metal if the atoms are constantly disturbed by hammer blows or by being heated. (Heat makes a metal's atoms vibrate more vigorously.) The opposite is also true. Heating a magnet or repeatedly striking it with a hammer "shakes up" the atomic magnets. They take on a random arrangement again, and the magnet loses its magnetism.

Objects left for a long period near a magnet can become magnetized. The loudspeakers of audio equipment contain strong permanent magnets. Small metal objects such as screws can become magnetized if they are left a long time near speakers. Being left near speakers can spoil audiotapes (on which sound is recorded as a pattern of magnetization in the metal coating on a plastic tape) because the magnetization is altered. Stray magnetic fields also affect other types of magnetic storage device, but not those in which the storage mechanism is solid-state (e.g., memory sticks).

TRY THIS

Captive filings

Once a piece of special steel is magnetized, it tends to stay magnetized. It becomes a permanent magnet, and its magnetic field cannot be turned on and off. However, an electromagnet can be turned on and off, and anything attracted to it becomes its slave, to come to it when bidden. In this project, you will make some iron filings jump when an electromagnet makes them do so.

What to do

Use the point of a nail to punch a hole through the center of a piece of thick cardboard about 6 in (15 cm) square. Wind a length of wire around and around the nail, leaving about 1 ft (30 cm) of wire free at each end. Thread one end of the wire through the hole in the cardboard, push in the nail, and stand it on a reel of tape so that the cardboard is flat and the nail is upright (see the illustration). Sprinkle iron filings thinly on the cardboard around the nail. Connect the ends of the wires to the terminals of a battery, and watch what happens to the iron filings. Disconnect one wire. (Do not leave it connected for long as the wires and the nail will get hot.) The iron filings form a pattern like a star around the nail, which is acting as an electromagnet. When you disconnect one wire, the filings are no longer attracted by the electromagnet and can be shuffled about. But as soon as you reconnect the wire to the battery, the filings immediately jump back into their pattern.

Iron filings reveal the starlike pattern of the electromagnet's field.

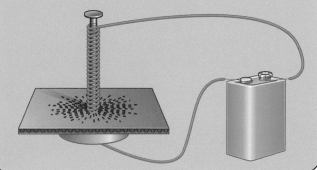

USES OF MAGNETS

Magnets, often working hand in hand with electricity, are essential in recording, transmitting, and receiving data in audio, TV, and computer systems. In industry, they do heavy work, while in medicine they reveal the workings of our bodies.

Magnets are used in devices all around us. One important use is in computers. Computer hard disks are coated with magnetic material. Data is stored in this coating by a moving arm called a read–write head, which applies a magnetic field to the disk to make a tiny magnetized area, corresponding to a bit. (A bit is a 0 or a 1, the basic units of information as used in connection with computers and digital communications.) The read–write head can also read information already on the disk by detecting the magnetization of the surface directly beneath the head.

MAGNETIC STORAGE

A kind of magnetic storage that is built into every personal computer is the hard drive, which uses one or more hard disks. Until the late 1990s, most PCs also incorporated a "floppy" disk drive, using a single flexible magnetic disk. These have now been replaced by USB flash drives, CD-ROM and DVD drives, which are nonmagnetic.

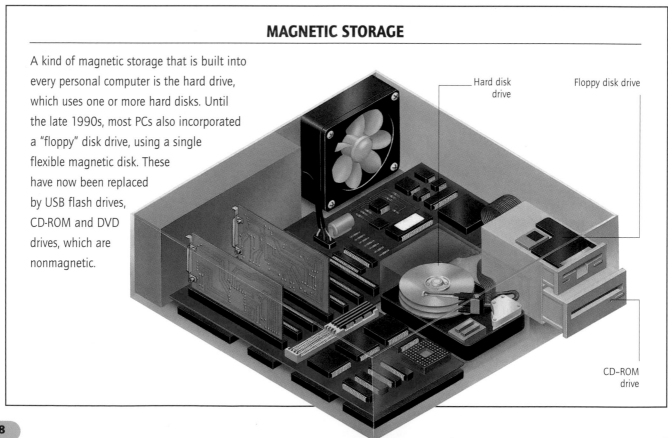

Hard disk drive

Floppy disk drive

CD-ROM drive

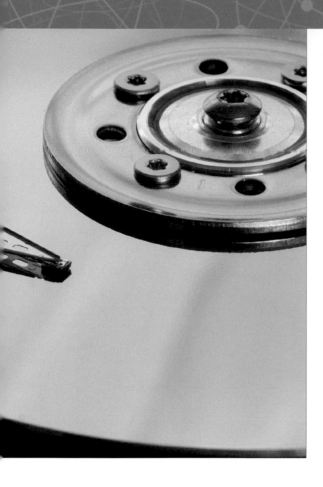

A computer's hard disk drive contains two or more rigid metal platters coated with a magnetic material. Read-write heads swing back and forth across each platter as it spins rapidly.

Some large mainframe computers, which are needed to store the large quantities of information required by, say, major corporations, universities, or the military, also use magnetic tapes. These consist of plastic film with a coating of a magnetic material. The same principle is used in audiotapes and videotapes for storing information representing sounds and pictures.

A magnetic signal is recorded onto a magnetic disk or tape by applying a fluctuating magnetic field. A varying electric current flowing through an electromagnet in the recording head creates this field. When the magnetic signal is read, the fluctuations in the magnetism of the recording surface as it speeds past the detector generate a varying electric current in the detector. This current is then amplified to give the output.

TRY THIS

How attractive?

A magnet attracts some materials, but not others. In this project, you will examine various materials and discover which are attracted and which are not.

What to do

Collect various objects to test, such as a pin, coins, an eraser, a piece of aluminum foil, a wax crayon, and a thumbtack. Touch each object in turn with the magnet, and note which objects are attracted to it. You could put those that are attracted to it in one pile and those that are not in another pile. Do the attracted objects have anything in common?

If you look at the attracted objects, you will see that they are all made of steel. Objects made of other metals, such as copper coins, nickels, and aluminum foil, were not attracted. So it's not just any metallic object, only steel ones that are attracted, and these objects themselves become magnetized. Notice that none of the nonmetallic objects were attracted by the magnet.

Use a magnet to try to pick up objects made from a variety of materials.

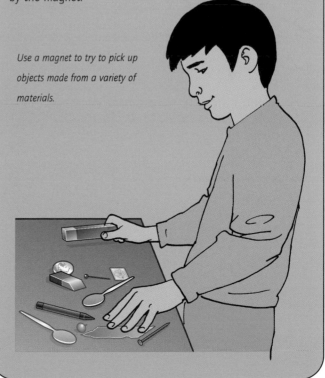

Magnetic pictures

Modern medicine now relies heavily on the ability to create images of organs inside the living human body. There are several techniques for doing this, and one of the most important is magnetic resonance imaging (MRI).

When a patient has an MRI scan, he or she lies down and is positioned with the relevant part of the body, such as the head or chest, in the scanner. A powerful magnetic field, tens of thousands of times as strong as the Earth's field, is turned on. The patient's body is then bathed in radio waves. The magnetic field puts the hydrogen atoms in the patient's tissues into a state in which they can absorb energy from the radio waves. When the signals are turned off, these hydrogen atoms reradiate the energy they have absorbed. Detectors pick up these "broadcasts," and a powerful computer assembles the signals into a multicolored image of the interior of the body. The brightness and color of each part of the image represent the amount

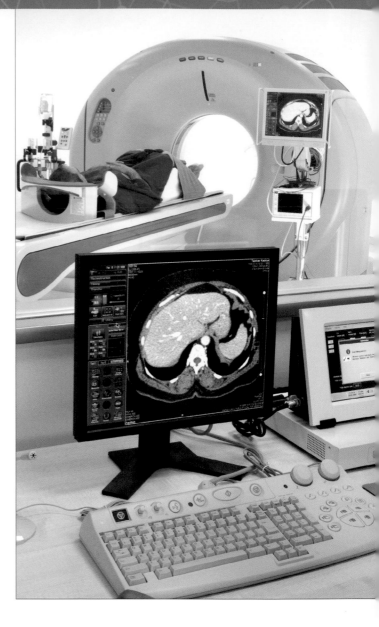

An MRI scanner uses a powerful magnetic field and radio waves to make hydrogen atoms in the patient's body "broadcast" their own radio signals, from which a computer can build up an image of the patient's internal organs.

and type of tissue present at the corresponding point in the body.

A technique called functional MRI (fMRI) can show how much activity is going on in a person's internal organs—for example, the activity of the parts of the brain that are involved in emotional reactions or in tasks such as mental arithmetic.

SCIENCE WORDS

- **Electromagnet:** A device that develops a magnetic field when electric current is passed through it. It consists of a coil with a core.
- **Magnetic resonance imaging (MRI):** The technique of making pictures of the inside of, for example, the living human body. A person is placed in a strong magnetic field and bathed in radio waves. Hydrogen atoms in the body reveal themselves by "rebroadcasting" the waves.
- **Superconductivity:** The property of conducting electricity with no resistance at all. Some metals do this when cooled to a temperature close to absolute zero (−459.67°F/−273.15°C). New complex substances have been developed that superconduct at ever higher temperatures (though not yet as high as 32°F/0°C)).

Heavy lifting

Electromagnets are important in industry. They are magnets in which the magnetism is generated by electric current. The magnetic field can be much stronger than is possible in solid permanent magnets, and it can be switched on and off simply by switching the current on and off (see pages 24–27). Strong electromagnets are used in cranes for lifting iron and steel objects, such as junked vehicles at wrecking yards.

They can also be used for separating metal ores and scrap metal. This is an essential preliminary to processing the material to get a high level of purity in the metal that is refined from the ore or recovered from the scrap. The materials to be separated are dropped onto a drum rotating around a semicircular electromagnet. Any nonmagnetic materials drop off into a bin. The drum holds magnetic materials as it rotates until they pass the magnet, when they fall into a separate container.

Guiding particles

Scientists learn about the structure of matter by accelerating subatomic particles in giant machines called colliders and then smashing the particles into one another. Two such machines share an enormous circular underground tunnel 17 miles (27 km) in circumference at CERN, the European Laboratory for Particle Physics, near Geneva in Switzerland. To keep the particles, traveling at almost the speed of light, on the curved path, they have to be held on course by electromagnets that encircle the path of the particle beams. The electromagnets have to be very powerful, and for this purpose superconductors are used. They are metals kept at low temperatures so that they become superconducting—that is, they pass electric currents without offering any electrical resistance and therefore lose almost no energy as wasted heat.

Magnetic fields are also important in the detectors that record the paths of particles produced in the collisions. A magnetic field forces the electrically charged particles to follow curved paths. The amount of curvature depends on the speed of the particle and on

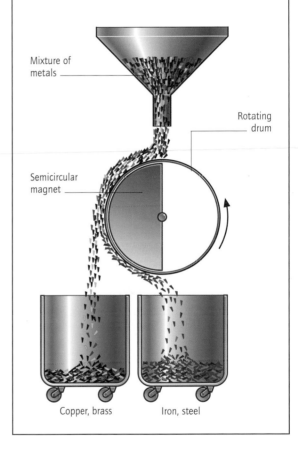

MAGNETIC SEPARATOR

Magnetic and nonmagnetic scrap metals can be separated from each other by means of a rotating drum and an electromagnet. Copper and brass are among the metals that simply slide off the drum. Iron, steel, and other magnetic metals stick to its surface until they pass the magnet and fall off.

Mixture of metals

Rotating drum

Semicircular magnet

Copper, brass   Iron, steel

its mass. So, a magnetic field is generated in a particle detector to bend the paths of the particles produced. Measuring the curvatures of the paths that appear in the pictures provides important data on the particles.

Magnetic fields also bend the paths of particles in TV sets. Electromagnets in the picture tube force a beam of electrons to sweep from side to side and from top to bottom of the screen, making dots of phosphorescent material glow and form a picture.

For nearly 200 years, scientists have known that electricity and magnetism are closely interlinked. Electric currents generate magnetic fields; and magnetic fields, when they alter, can drive electric currents. Scientists now regard electricity and magnetism as two aspects of a single phenomenon, which is called electromagnetism.

The link between electricity and magnetism was first discovered quite early in the 19th century. The Danish physicist Hans Christian Oersted (1777–1851) found that a wire carrying an electric current will affect a magnetic needle. The magnetic field lines around a wire are circles. If you look along a wire, and the current is flowing toward you, the field lines (the direction of the force on a north magnetic pole) go in a counterclockwise sense, as shown in diagram (a) opposite (page 23). (Throughout this book the direction of an electric current is defined as the direction of flow of positive charge. Actually, the current consists of negatively charged electrons moving in the opposite

MAGNETIC FIELDS OF CURRENTS

The magnetic field lines around a current-carrying wire are circular. With current flowing downward into a surface, the field lines run clockwise as seen from above. The fields of nearby currents combine in the patterns shown here. When the currents in two parallel wires are in the same direction, the wires attract each other. When they are in opposite directions, the wires repel each other.

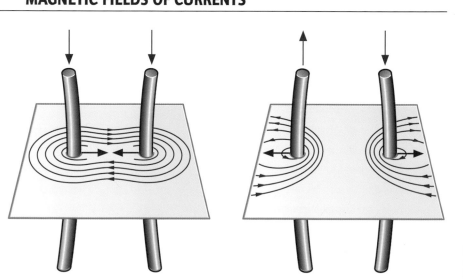

Metal detectors at airports guard against concealed weapons and bombs in baggage or passengers' clothing. The devices respond to the magnetic effects of metal objects.

direction, but this does not really matter.)

This looks very different from the shape of the field of a bar magnet or of the Earth. But if the wire is coiled into a single loop, the shape of the field begins to resemble that of a bar magnet (b, at right). And if the wire is looped into many turns to form a cylindrical coil, called a solenoid (c and d, at right), the fields of all the loops combine to make a stronger field, and the field lines strongly resemble those of a bar magnet.

In fact, the field of a magnetic material is created by countless tiny electric currents in the atoms of metal forming myriad tiny magnets, which act in unison to form the one big magnet.

The magnetic fields of electric currents interact with each other just as the magnetic fields of magnets do. The result is that electric currents attract and repel one another. As shown in the illustration on the left (page 22), currents flowing in the same direction in two neighboring wires attract each other, while currents flowing in opposite directions repel each other. And solenoids behave just like bar magnets in this way, too: each has a north-seeking and a south-seeking end, or pole, and like poles repel while unlike ones attract.

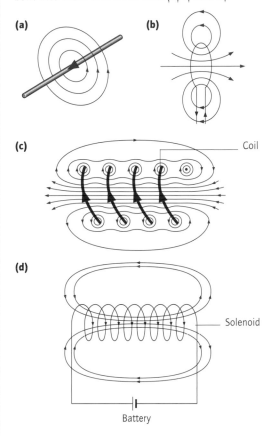

CURRENT-CARRYING COILS

The field of a current (a) becomes more and more like that of a bar magnet as the wire is bent into more and more coils (b, c, and d).

(a)

(b)

(c)   Coil

(d)

Solenoid

Battery

SCIENCE WORDS

- **Electromagnetism:** The interlinked phenomena of electricity and magnetism. Every electric current generates a magnetic field, while changes in a magnetic field can cause a current to flow.
- **Solenoid:** A current-carrying coil of wire. When a current flows through a solenoid, a magnetic field is developed in it. Often there is a moving iron core in the coil that moves when it is attracted by the magnetic field.

ELECTROMAGNETS

Electricity may be used to generate powerful magnetic fields that can be turned on and off at the flick of a switch. Electromagnets are valuable in industry, and the principle behind them is applied in countless other devices, many familiar in the home.

Coiling a current-carrying wire into a solenoid makes it into an electromagnet. This is a very convenient type of magnet because it can be switched on and off. The strength of its magnetism depends on

THE PRINCIPLE OF THE ELECTROMAGNET

A core of iron concentrates the field of a current-carrying solenoid, but it loses almost all of its magnetization when the current is switched off.

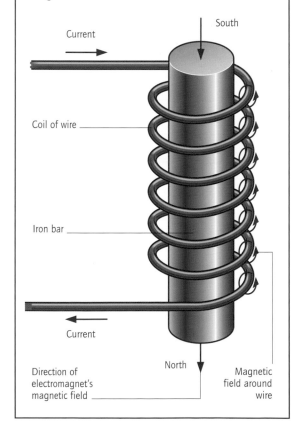

Current

South

Coil of wire

Iron bar

Current

North

Direction of electromagnet's magnetic field

Magnetic field around wire

---

the strength of the current passing through it. However, the amount of current is limited by the heating effect that it causes.

An electromagnet can be made more powerful by wrapping the wire around a central core of iron. It becomes strongly magnetized by the magnetic field of the solenoid, which greatly strengthens the total field of the magnet. As the strength of the current is increased, the magnetization of the iron increases until it reaches a maximum—it becomes saturated (see pages 4–5). Increasing the current further increases the

The Compact Muon Solenoid, part of the Large Hadron Collider experiment at CERN in Geneva, incorporates a massive electromagnet 42 ft (13 m) long and almost 20 ft (6 m) in diameter. This solenoid's refrigerated coils are made from a niobium-titanium alloy.

field only by the amount contributed by the solenoid's own direct field. Whatever material is used in the electromagnet's core, it needs to be "soft," which means that it is able to lose magnetism as readily as it gains it.

The current required to power an electromagnet can come from any of several different sources. In portable

TRY THIS

Testing an electromagnet
In this project you will test a simple electromagnet to see if you can make it stronger.

What to do
Wind a 4-ft (1.3-m) length of insulated wire around and around a steel nail about 4–6 in (10–15 cm) long, leaving about 1 ft (30 cm) of wire free at each end. Connect the free ends to the terminals of a 9-volt battery. To test the strength of this electromagnet, see how many paper clips it will pick up. (Do not leave it connected to the battery for too long because the wires and the nail will get hot.)

Now wind a piece of insulated wire twice as long around another nail, again leaving about 1 ft (30 cm) of wire free at each end. Again, connect it to a battery and see how many paper clips it will pick up. (And again, do not leave it connected to the battery for too long.) Did it pick up more clips or fewer clips than the first electromagnet?

Finally, try powering each electromagnet with two batteries. (And don't leave either electromagnet connected to the batteries for too long.)

Which electromagnet picked up the most paper clips? Were the electromagnets that had two batteries more powerful than the electromagnet with only one battery? You should find that the greater the number of turns of wire, the more powerful the electromagnet. Also, the higher the voltage, the more powerful the electromagnet.

A higher voltage produces a more powerful electromagnet.

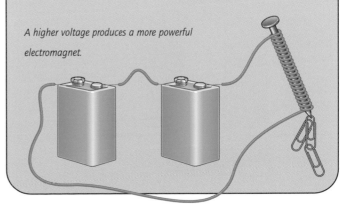

Joseph Henry

The American physicist Joseph Henry was born in 1797. He discovered the principle of electromagnetic induction—that changing electric currents in one circuit can cause currents to be generated in another circuit. However, he did not get the credit for the discovery because the British physicist Michael Faraday (1791–1867) announced the results of his own independent studies on the subject before Henry did. Henry developed improved electromagnets and built one of the first electric motors. He also invented one of the first successful electric telegraphs, for which he developed the relay, allowing messages to be sent over long distances without them growing fainter. In 1846, Henry became first director of the newly formed Smithsonian Institution in Washington, D.C., and served in that position until his death in 1878. He developed the study of meteorology at the Smithsonian and pioneered weather forecasting. The unit of electrical inductance is named in his honor.

PRINCIPLE OF HENRY'S ELECTROMAGNET

Coils magnetize the two legs of the horseshoe magnet. The magnetism in each leg induces a magnetic pole at each end of a piece of iron placed across the horseshoe's poles.

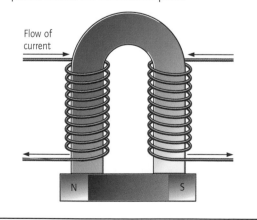

Flow of current

N   S

devices such as electric razors, batteries do the job. On motor vehicles, ships, and airplanes the vehicle's own engine or engines generate an electrical supply that powers all the systems, including those that incorporate electromagnets. In homes, offices, and factories the electricity supply is the source of current (see pages 28–31). In some of the first experiments to study electromagnets the U.S. physicist Joseph Henry (1797–1878) used a primitive electric cell, or battery. It consisted of plates of two different kinds of metal, such as copper and zinc, dipping into acid. Using hundreds of turns of insulated wire, Henry made electromagnets that could lift over a ton.

Peril on the sea

One of the strangest ever applications of the electromagnet has been in wartime to protect ships against magnetic mines. Magnetic mines float beneath the surface of the sea, tethered to the sea floor. When a ship passes nearby, the metal of the ship is detected by a sensitive magnetic needle in the mine. The swinging needle acts as the moving part of an electric switch. If a nearby ship makes the needle swing, the switch is closed. Current from a battery flows through an electric detonator, exploding the mine and damaging or even sinking the ship.

The mine is triggered because the ship is a giant magnet, though a weak one, with a magnetic field induced by long exposure to the Earth's magnetic field. Degaussing belts—cables that encircle the ship's hull and carry electric current—generate a magnetic field opposite to that of the ship and in this way counteract the ship's own magnetism.

Beam-benders

Electric currents are not confined to those that flow in wires. They also flow through free space. In a cathode-ray TV picture tube a beam of electrons travels from a heated cathode at the rear to sweep across the screen and illuminate tiny phosphor dots on the screen to form a picture. Beams of electrons are also used in

A scanning electron microscope (SEM) in operation. SEMs, which are often used to analyse the surface structure of materials, can give a magnification up to 250 times the limit of the best optical microscopes.

electron microscopes, instruments that can see details far smaller than can be seen with optical microscopes using ordinary light. One type of electron microscope,

SCIENCE WORDS

- **Horseshoe magnet:** A permanent magnet that is bent into a horseshoe shape so that the two poles are close together, and their strengths combine.
- **Magnetic lens**: An arrangement of electromagnets that can focus a beam of electrons or other charged particles, as in an electron microscope.
- **Magnetization:** The process of making an object or material into a magnet.

ELECTRON MICROSCOPE

The electron microscope uses a beam of electrons in place of a beam of light. The electrons, like all subatomic particles, have a wavelength that is much shorter than that of light, thus making it possible to form extremely detailed images. The electron beam, traveling from the top of the instrument downward, is focused by strong "magnetic lenses," which are current-carrying coils.

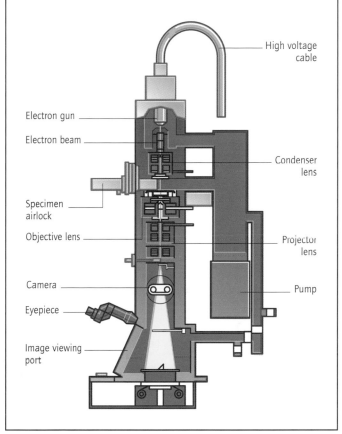

the transmission electron microscope, or TEM, can see details the size of individual atoms. The electrons are accelerated by hundreds of thousands of volts. (The electron beam current may be only a billionth of an amp, compared with about half an amp in the current going through a typical desk lamp bulb.) The electron beam is shaped, focused, and guided by electromagnets consisting of current-carrying coils through which the beam passes on the way to its target.

ELECTROMAGNETIC DEVICES

We live in a push-button world—we consider it normal that the press of a finger is enough to lift mighty weights or carry our words around the world. All this is made possible by putting electromagnetism to work.

The discovery of electromagnetism by scientists in the early 19th century led to a steady stream of inventions that depended on the principle of electric currents and magnetic fields interacting with each other. The stream grew into a flood, and today we are surrounded by electromagnetic devices in daily life. The American physicist Joseph Henry (1797–1878) made one of the earliest such innovations in 1831, when he built the first electric bell. The bell was struck repeatedly by a clapper that was held away from the bell by a spring when no current flowed. Pressing a

The electric bell creates its characteristic high-pitched trilling noise by the action of a hammer striking the bell rapidly and repeatedly. The hammer vibrates because it is pulled one way by an electromagnet and the other way by a mechanical spring.

button allowed electric current to flow in the circuit through a solenoid. The magnetic field generated by the solenoid attracted the metal arm of the clapper, which struck the bell. But the movement of the clapper also broke the circuit so that the current ceased and the magnetic field disappeared. The clapper, no longer attracted, jumped back and closed the circuit. As long as the button was pressed, this cycle repeated itself.

The electric bell was much more convenient than the pull-cord bell then in use. Electric wires could be run from room to room more easily than pull-cords and could be made to sound more than one bell if needed. Bells could be very loud and have a variety of tones. Variants, such as chimes, could easily be provided.

Samuel Morse

Samuel Finley Breese Morse was born in Charlestown, Massachusetts in 1791. After graduating from Yale in 1810, he went to England to study art before returning home five years later and setting himself up as a portrait painter. In the 1830s, his interest turned to electricity; he was inspired to invent the electric telegraph after meeting Joseph Henry (1797–1878), who showed him that the arrival of an electric current along a

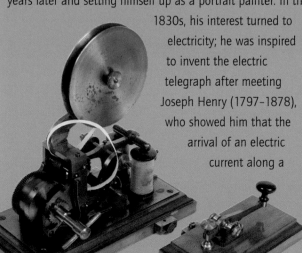

wire could be detected by making it work an electromagnet. When the current arrived, the magnet pulled over an iron armature with an audible "click." In 1843, Morse built a 37-mile (60-km) telegraph line from Washington, D.C. to Baltimore and the following year sent the world's first message ("What hath God wrought!") by telegraph. Essential to this technology's success was Morse code, a system of short and long electrical pulses ("dots" and "dashes") that encode the letters of the alphabet. The code was devised by Morse and his assistant Alfred Vail (1807–1859), with the shortest codes being assigned to the commonest letters in English. Morse died in New York City in 1872.

An electric telegraph key (left) and receiver (far left). As the pulses were registered by the receiver, it marked the dots and dashes of the message on a paper tape.

Pressing the doorbell sends a pulse of current through the solenoid, making the iron rod jerk across sharply and hit one of the chimes. Instantly a spring (not shown) pulls it back again, striking the second chime.

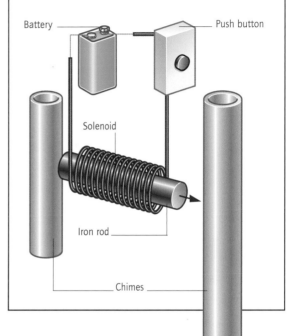

Battery   Push button

Solenoid

Iron rod

Chimes

The telegraph

An early use of electromagnetism was in the electric telegraph. Messages could be sent long distances by wire in the form of long and short pulses of electric current. These pulses deflected a recording pen at the receiving end. Short electric pulses were registered as dots, and long pulses as dashes. Combinations of dots and dashes stood for letters of the alphabet according to a code devised by the US inventor Samuel Morse (1791–1872).

To send signals over long distances, it was necessary to overcome the weakening of signals as they passed over telegraph wires many miles long. Electromagnetism was put to use again with the invention of the relay. The signals in each stretch of telegraph wire, roughly 20 miles (32 km) long, were used to open and close switches in the next stretch of the wire, which had its own electricity supply. In this way, signals could be sent for unlimited distances without loss of strength.

This principle is still important today. A relay is a device that enables the current in one circuit to control the current in another. The second current may be large and therefore dangerous, while the first one is small and safe to operate, as when a truck driver brings an engine to life with a powerful current from the battery, controlled by a weak current that is switched on with the turn of the ignition key.

Car devices

Apart from the starter relay and other relays, the modern car is packed with electrical devices in which magnetism plays a key role. Many devices are actually small motors, and they are discussed in detail later (pages 34-37). There are also a variety of magnetic sensors. One detects the position of the throttle (in cars that have cruise control, which keeps a constant throttle setting without foot pressure for freeway

driving). Another sensor detects the position of the steering wheel in cars with power steering, so that the amount of power that is delivered to help turn the wheel can be controlled precisely.

Electromagnetism and sound

Magnetism is vital in sound reproduction. Relatively weak electric currents, varying in strength many thousands of times per second, drive loudspeakers in a radio, CD player, or TV set. The pattern of the current—the audio signal—is a copy of the pattern of loudness of the voices, music, or other sounds that the current might be representing.

This varying current is passed through a solenoid called the voice coil, attached to the center of a paper or plastic cone. The coil is in the field of a strong permanent magnet that may take the form of, say, a ring surrounding the coil. The varying current gives rise to a constantly fluctuating magnetic field generated by the coil, and the coil is pulled by the permanent magnet with a strength that depends on the current. The coil vibrates, along with the cone attached to it. The vibrating cone disturbs the air, setting up sound waves that are exact copies of the original ones.

A microphone originally produces the electric current that carries the audio signal. In the most important types of microphone, once again it is electromagnetism that plays a key role. The vibrations

STARTER MOTOR

A car is equipped with an electric starter motor, which is turned by a large current delivered to it by the car's battery. This current is turned on by the starter relay, in which a low current from the battery activates a solenoid when the driver turns the key in the ignition switch.

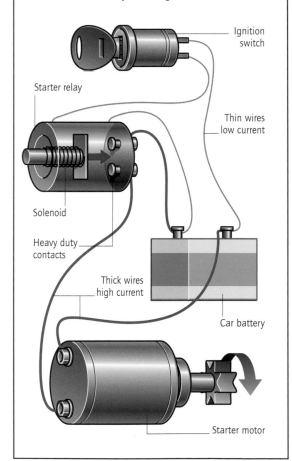

Ignition switch

Starter relay

Thin wires low current

Solenoid

Heavy duty contacts

Thick wires high current

Car battery

Starter motor

of sounds that strike the microphone cause a light plastic diaphragm to vibrate. Attached to the diaphragm is a metal ribbon or coil in the field of a permanent magnet. As the metal vibrates in the field, the effect is the same as if the magnet were being moved while the metal remained still: a voltage is induced in the metal. This creates the small audio current.

After World War I, new types of electromagnetic microphones and loudspeakers were developed. The first sound-recording machines had speaking-tubes for microphones and large horns to amplify the faint sounds produced by the needle as it ran along the groove of a recording disk or cylinder. Electronic reproduction of sound proved more accurate, allowing a greater range of frequencies and greater volume when required.

Speakers, such as this amplifier, contain a strong permanent magnet and a coil acting as an electromagnet. The interaction between them makes the cone in the speaker vibrate and generate sound.

THE RELAY

A relay is a device by which the current in one circuit controls the current in another. In the design shown here a switch in a low-current circuit controls a motor that draws a large current. Closing the switch in the lower circuit allows a low current to pass, so that the solenoid generates a magnetic field. That attracts the pivoted armature, allowing a strong AC current to flow in the second circuit, operating the motor.

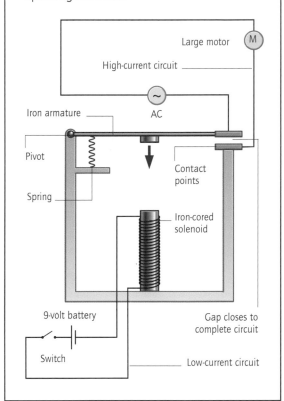

Large motor — M
High-current circuit
AC
Iron armature
Pivot
Contact points
Spring
Iron-cored solenoid
9-volt battery
Gap closes to complete circuit
Switch
Low-current circuit

Electromagnetism was used in a different way to revolutionize a musical instrument. Magnetic detectors called pickups were added to the steel-stringed guitar so that the vibrations of the strings were turned directly into electrical signals. They could be amplified (made stronger) or altered in various ways and then fed into a loudspeaker. This new power enabled the guitar to play a more prominent role in dance bands and jazz groups.

MOTOR EFFECT

Magnetic fields produced by permanent magnets or electric currents can move current-carrying wires. Early researchers studied this effect and designed the first electric motors. Their laboratory toys grew into the workhorses of modern industry.

After Oersted's ground-breaking discovery of 1819, the British physicist Michael Faraday (1791–1867) made the most thorough experimental investigation of the interactions between electricity and magnetism. The French physicist André Ampère (1775–1836) had found that not only did current-carrying wires produce magnetic fields, they also experienced forces when they were placed in magnetic fields, making them seem even more similar to magnets.

Michael Faraday (left) pictured in his laboratory with fellow scientist John Daniell, inventor of a battery that bears his name (see page 59).

Faraday announced his "left-hand motor rule" as a reminder of how these forces acted. Imagine that the thumb, first finger, and second finger of your left hand are extended at right angles to one another:

- if the first finger represents the direction of the field
- and the second finger represents the direction of the current
- then the thumb represents the direction of movement of the current-carrying wire.

(As always in this book, the direction of the current is taken to be the direction of flow of positive charge, the opposite of the direction of flow of the negatively charged electrons.)

A primitive motor

Faraday set up a very striking demonstration of the effect of the interaction between current and

---

MOTOR EFFECT DEMONSTRATION

When current flows through the copper rod dipping in the mercury, the rod revolves around the magnet.

Battery

Copper rod

Magnet

Mercury

magnetism. He let a current flow through a freely suspended copper rod that was dipping in a pool of the liquid metal mercury (a good conductor). When a bar magnet was placed upright near the rod, the rod started to revolve around the magnet and kept revolving for as long as the current flowed. Because the current was roughly vertical and the magnetic field lines went to and from the magnet, there was a force on the rod at right angles to both of them—that is, around the circumference of a circle.

If a current is passed through a coil in a magnetic field, the two sides of the coil experience forces in opposite directions (because the current flows in opposite directions on the two sides of the coil). This creates a torque, or twisting force, on the coil (except when it is exactly at right angles to the field lines, when the forces tend to stretch or squeeze the coil, but not turn it). The more turns the coil has, the stronger the current, and the stronger the magnetic field, the stronger the force on it. This was to be the basis of the powerful electric motors of today.

SCIENCE WORDS

- **Coil:** A spiral of wire through which current flows. The magnetic fields of the current in the different turns of the coil add together to make a large magnetic field. The coil is then an electromagnet, with a field resembling that of a bar magnet.
- **Left-hand motor rule:** When the directions of a magnetic field and electric current are represented by the first and second fingers respectively of the left hand, the direction of motion of the current-carrying conductor is indicated by the thumb when all three digits are extended at right angles to one another.
- **Torque:** Any force or system of forces that cause rotation.

MAGNETIC FORCE ON A CURRENT

Faraday showed that a current-carrying wire experiences an upward force when the current and magnetic field are in the directions shown here.

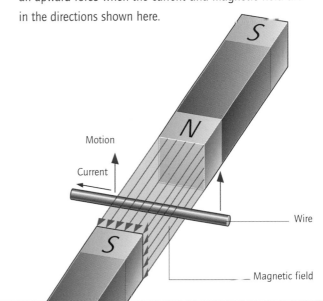

MAGNETIC FORCE ON A COIL

A current-carrying coil in a magnetic field tends to rotate until it is at right angles to the field lines. (a) The interaction between the magnetic field and the current causes the coil to turn. (b) When the coil is at right angles to the field, there is no turning force.

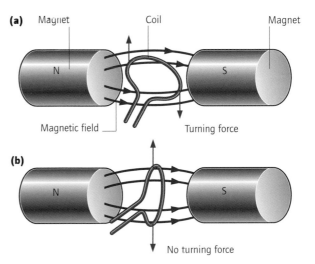

ELECTRIC MOTORS

Our civilization would collapse were it not for electric motors. There are many designs, each intended to do a particular job, from small motors in electric clocks to large winding motors for a skyscraper's elevators. They depend on ingenious engineering that exploits the intimate connection between electricity and magnetism.

The simple rotating coil shown on the previous page has to be made considerably more complicated to turn it into an electric motor. Yet the basic principle remains the same in all motors: an electric current moving through a magnetic field experiences a force at right angles to itself and to the field. The force can be turned into movement, and the movement can be made to do useful work such as moving a vehicle, or raising a weight, or opening a door.

THE DC MOTOR

Direct current (DC) is a steady current that does not vary with time. In the simplest sort of electric motor,

SCIENCE WORDS

- **AC motor:** An electric motor that is operated by alternating current.
- **Alternating current (AC):** Electric current that flows first in one direction, then in the other, alternating many times each second. AC is used for domestic electricity supply and many other electrical applications.
- **DC motor:** An electric motor that is operated by direct current.
- **Direct current (DC):** Electric current that flows in one direction all the time, though it may vary in strength.

direct current is passed through a coil of many turns that is free to rotate in the field of a permanent magnet. In the upper illustration on the opposite page, current flowing away from you experiences an upward force. With the coil in the position shown, the torque is

A small electric induction motor. Clearly visible on either side of the spindle, are the wound copper coils in the motor's stator. When these are supplied with power, they create a rotating magnetic field pattern that in turn induces current in the rotor conductors, so causing the rotor to turn.

DC MOTOR

The magnetic field forces the current-carrying coil to rotate. Attached to the coil is the split-ring commutator, which reverses the current at every half-turn.

Direction coil moves

Direction of rotation

Flow of current through coil

N

Brush

S

Coil

Magnet

Brush

Spring-ring commutator

therefore clockwise. When the plane of the coil is parallel to the field, like this, the torque (twisting force) on the coil is at its maximum.

When the coil has turned through 90 degrees from this position, there is no torque on it, but its momentum carries it past this point. If the flow of current were not altered, the torque on the coil would now be counterclockwise, tending to slow down the rotation. To prevent this, the current is reversed when the coil is at 90 degrees to the field. The current is supplied through a commutator—a cylinder split into two parts, each part touching one brush, or contact. As the coil turns to the 90-degree position, each half of the commutator comes into contact with the other brush, reversing the direction of flow into the coil. So the coil gets an increasing twist in the same direction as it turns through the next 90 degrees. When it has turned to the point where it is once again at right angles to the field, the current is again reversed.

AC MOTOR

The direction of the current reverses continually, ensuring that the coil always experiences a turning force in the same direction.

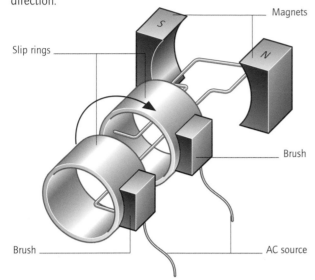

Magnets

Slip rings

Brush

Brush

AC source

INDUCTION MOTOR

AC current flowing in the coils of the stator (the outer assembly) generates a rotating magnetic field that drags the rotor around.

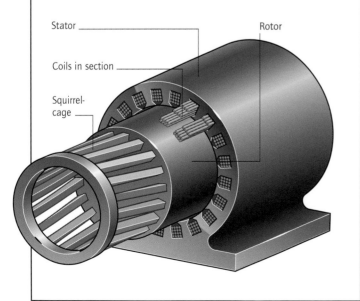

Stator

Rotor

Coils in section

Squirrel-cage

SCIENCE WORDS

- **Induction motor:** An electric motor in which a moving magnetic field induces (generates) current in another component, which moves to follow the field. The moving part may revolve or move in a straight line. See also Linear induction motor.
- **Linear induction motor:** An induction motor that produces straight-line motion, as, for example, in making a sliding door close and open.
- **Stator:** The stationary part of a motor or generator.

The AC motor

An AC motor can in principle be simpler than this, as in the diagram on the left. Because alternating current reverses itself periodically (the electricity supply goes through 60 cycles per second in the United States), there is no need for a commutator if the coil revolves at this rate. Such a motor will adjust its rate automatically to the frequency of the supplied current.

However, all practical motors have to be more complicated than these examples. The magnetic field is likely to be supplied by electromagnets rather than a permanent magnet. The power supply to the motor sends some current through coils called field magnets around the outside of the motor in an assembly called the stator. There can be many rotating coils, making up an assembly called the rotor. It is supplied with current through a commutator divided into a corresponding number of segments, so that at any moment current flows into the coil that is in the plane of the field and so produces the maximum torque.

The induction motor

The most common type of AC motor is the induction motor, which works on a different principle from the one described above. In an induction motor, AC current is passed through field coils in a stator, one coil after another, so that viewed from one end, the direction of the magnetic field rotates. Housed within the stator is a structure called a squirrel-cage, which consists of bars of iron or other soft magnetic metal. The revolving field in the stator induces a magnetic field in the squirrel-cage (hence the name "induction motor"). The squirrel-cage moves around with the field.

The linear induction motor

A similar principle can be used in motors that move objects in straight lines. In the linear induction motor, field coils are arranged along a track. A pulse of current passes through successive coils in turn, sending a wave of magnetism along the track. A flat plate of suitable metal laid on or alongside the track has magnetism induced in it and moves along with the wave. Linear induction motors are widely used for sliding doors and in some other machines, such as the shuttles of looms, where straight-line motion is required.

LINEAR INDUCTION MOTOR

If an induction motor (a) were imagined to be "unrolled" (b), it would form a linear induction motor (c). Traveling magnetic fields in the track pull the metal plate along.

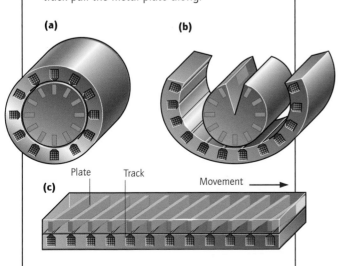

(a)

(b)

(c) Plate   Track   Movement →

PRACTICAL DC MOTOR

The magnetic field is provided not by a permanent magnet, but by current passing through field magnet windings. The commutator has many segments, corresponding to the number of field magnet coils in the armature.

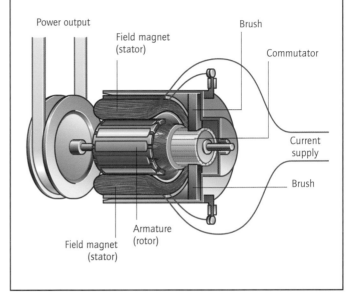

Power output

Field magnet (stator)

Brush

Commutator

Current supply

Brush

Armature (rotor)

Field magnet (stator)

Motors everywhere

In industrialized countries, electric motors are present everywhere, running countless details of our lives where we might not suspect their presence. A car, for example, is a good place to find them. Small electric motors drive windshield wipers and washers, electric windows, sunroofs, centrally controlled door locks—and even adjustable rear-view mirrors, seats, and the extending radio antenna.

Domestic appliances—including dishwashers, washing machines, food-blenders, juicers, power drills, and vacuum cleaners—all rely on electric motors. Even a desktop computer has motors in it to power its disk drives and cooling fan. In factories, assembly lines, and a host of machines are driven by electric motors as well as transportation systems, such as trains, trams and cars. And every one of these electric motors relies on electromagnetism.

USING ELECTRIC MOTORS

The world generates most of its energy from coal, oil, gas, and nuclear fuel. A large fraction of this energy is converted into electricity and put to work by means of electric motors, which are everywhere around us.

Industrialization began in the 18th century with water power, applied in cotton mills and other factories. It was followed by steam power. The development of the electric motor in the 19th century carried industrialization into a new phase and made possible the development of many new devices. By 1850, experimental electric motors were powering boats and railroad locomotives.

Today, the sorts of jobs that electric motors have to do are very diverse. Some have to move large weights through large distances, such as those that raise large passenger elevators in tall office buildings. Others turn the hands on a watch. Some have to provide a smooth movement, such as the motors operating sliding doors; while with others, such as those in garbage-disposal units, the power that can be developed is more

important. Some must be very small, like those that must fit into a personal tape or CD player. With electric motors used in industry, size may be limited by the cost of large motors.

Ups and downs of modern life

The passenger elevator was made possible by the advent of the electric motor. A steam-operated passenger elevator had gone into service in a New York City department store in 1857. Although steam-operated and hydraulic elevators were successful, electrically powered ones took their place in the late

SCIENCE WORDS

● **Linear induction motor:** An induction motor that produces straight-line motion, as, for example, in making a sliding door close and open.
● **Pole:** One of the two regions of a magnet where the strength of the field is greatest. Lines of force diverge (radiate out) from one pole and converge on the other.
● **Rotor:** In electromagnetic technology the rotating coil in a motor or generator. See also Stator.
● **Stator:** The stationary part of a motor or generator. See also Rotor.

1880s. They were cleaner, quieter, more powerful, and more flexible, and types of motor were soon introduced that allowed the cars to be operated at a wide range of speeds without complicated gearing. The motors driving the fastest modern elevators can move them at 28 mph (45 km/h).

Tall modern buildings need so many elevators that designers are trying to get them to occupy smaller amounts of space. One way that is being explored is to take the motors away from the winding gear at the top of the shaft and replace them with flat linear induction motors built into the elevator car.

Stopping and starting

There are countless variations in the design of electric motors to deal with the differing circumstances in which they are used. There may be special adjustments to help them start slowly or prevent them from starting too quickly and violently.

The very first subway trains (in London) were driven by steam, which created major ventilation problems. But from the late 19th century on, electric traction became the norm in underground systems worldwide, as in this modern train on the Madrid Metro in Spain.

Current going to a motor's stator (pages 34–37) flows through the field coils, creating a magnetic field directed across the stator. In the simplest type of motor, called a two-pole motor, this field constantly reverses through 180 degrees because the supply is AC and so reverses continually. The rotor has its own magnetic field, which is produced either by a permanent magnet or by current. It swings around repeatedly, "trying" to bring its own north pole close to the south pole of the stator field, but never succeeding because the stator field is constantly switching. This kind of motor can be slow to get started. If, when the motor is switched on, the rotor field happens to be lined up with the stator field, then when the stator field flips, the rotor does not get a twist to one side or the other. Once the rotor is moving there is no problem—its own momentum carries it past this neutral position. Also, it can rotate equally well in either direction, so it has to be given an initial nudge in the right direction. Such a motor comes with an additional field coil and circuits that create an extra field when the device is started up; but once the motor is up to speed, they are disconnected automatically.

Often a motor has more than two poles—that is, more than one pair of field coils. As explained earlier (pages 34–37), current is sent to these pairs in succession to create a magnetic field that rotates, as seen from one end of the motor. This kind of motor generally has no startup problem.

In some kinds of motor there is a different kind of problem on starting. The motor is liable to start moving violently if full voltage is applied to it on switch-on. This would not be acceptable in streetcars and elevators, say, which must not jolt violently. Additional circuits are built into motors for such applications, which limit the field that is developed in the motor's rotor immediately after switch-on and are disconnected later.

FAN MOTOR

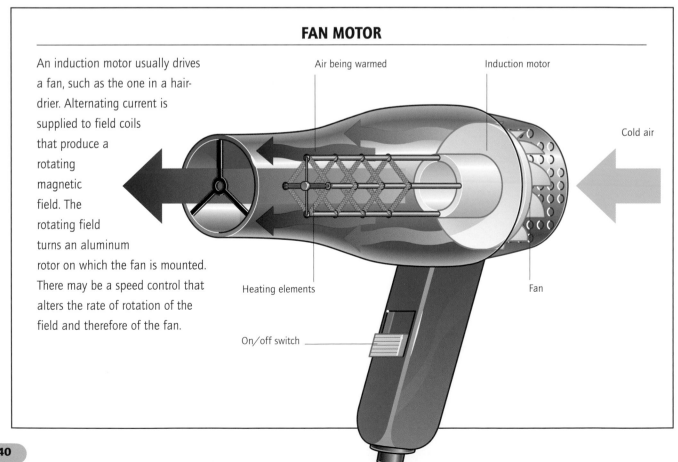

An induction motor usually drives a fan, such as the one in a hair-drier. Alternating current is supplied to field coils that produce a rotating magnetic field. The rotating field turns an aluminum rotor on which the fan is mounted. There may be a speed control that alters the rate of rotation of the field and therefore of the fan.

Air being warmed

Induction motor

Cold air

Heating elements

Fan

On/off switch

Electric motors have a wide range of applications in the home. Electric drills (right; dismantled to show its components) are usually equipped with a "universal" motor that can run on both AC and DC current. They generally have two speed settings. The drive unit in a DVD player (below) is precisely controlled to run between 200 and 500 rpm (revolutions per minute), depending on which track of the disk is being read.

Keeping steady

There are many applications in which it is important for the motor to turn at a steady speed. One is any kind of sound recording and playback, whether in a traditional phonograph turntable, or a CD or DVD drive. Another is in clocks and watches (the analog sort, which have hands). The AC supply from the power company is an ideal "pacemaker" for a motor because it is delivered at a constant frequency (60 cycles a second in the United States). If it is supplied to the stator of a motor, it will generate a field rotating 60 times a second. If the rotor is equipped with a permanent magnet, or with an

electromagnet supplied by a fixed-strength direct current, the rotor will follow the rotating field at the same rate. Such a motor is called "synchronous."

Motors used in watches and other portable devices clearly have to be very small. In the 1970s, it became possible to miniaturize components to the point where a motor could be compact yet powerful enough to power a personal tape-player, and the Sony Corporation marketed the Walkman, which later spawned a host of other personal audio devices.

ELECTRICITY FROM MACHINES

An electricity-generating plant is a place where energy of motion is turned into electrical energy. Monster machines and huge amounts of fuel are needed. With each year that passes, the electricity-supply industry is called on to deliver more energy to the expanding industries of the world.

In a power plant, turbines are spun by steam to generate electricity. The steam has to be produced by boiling purified water circulating in a closed system of pipes. Plants differ in the source of the heat they use to boil the water. Some burn coal; others, oil or gas; still others use heat from a nuclear reactor. A few use alternative forms of energy, such as sunlight or wave power, or heat from rocks deep beneath the ground.

The steam used in a conventional or nuclear power plant is superheated to temperatures of about 1000°F (550°C) or more. This steam is forced into the turbine, which consists of rotors, sets of rotating wheels equipped with fan blades, alternating with sets of fixed fan blades called stators. The steam's pressure forces the turbine's shaft to spin. The steam's temperature

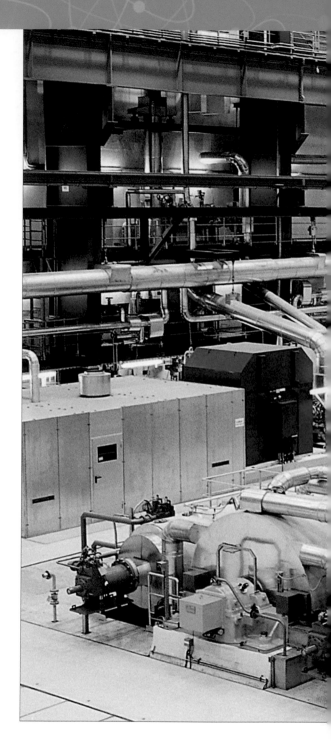

SCIENCE WORDS

- **Electromotive force (e.m.f.):** An electrical influence that tends to cause electric current to flow. E.m.f. is exerted by batteries and electric generators. It is measured in volts, and is also called potential difference or voltage.
- **Transformer:** A device that increases or decreases the voltage of alternating current.
- **Turbine:** A machine in which the energy of a moving fluid or air flow is converted into mechanical energy by causing a bladed rotor to rotate.

and pressure fall, but it is then led through lower-pressure stages of the turbine to extract as much energy as possible.

The last of the steam's heat is removed as it is circulated through pipes that are cooled by water from some external source, such as a lake or river. The condensed water is returned to be heated again.

The cooling water is returned to its source, though its possible effect on the environment must be carefully monitored and minimized. Warm water encourages the growth of algae, for example, which can cut down the oxygen available to fish. Clouds of water vapor can often be seen rising from the cooling towers that are a feature of many power plants.

Steam-driven turbines called turboalternators generate electricity. The main energy sources are coal, oil, gas, and nuclear energy.

The turbogenerator

From the steam turbine runs a shaft that spins at 3,600 rpm (in the United States) and is part of the generator. There is a strong magnetic field in the generator, which is produced by an independent supply of current flowing through electric coils called field windings. A complex structure called an armature, carrying electrical coils, spins in this magnetic field. An electromotive force of about 25,000 volts is generated.

Because the shaft rotates at 3,600 rpm, the current alternates at 60 Hz (that is, 60 hertz, or 60 times per second). This means that during $\frac{1}{120}$ second the number of electrons flowing in one direction increases and then decreases to zero; and then during the next $\frac{1}{120}$ second the flow builds up to a maximum in the reverse direction and then decreases to zero again. It is an alternating current (AC).

Stepping up

The power is delivered from the generator at about 25,000 volts. It is sent to a transformer, which steps up the voltage to several hundred thousand volts. This is necessary for sending power over long distances. The electrical cables have resistance, and heat is generated in them, which is wasted. Having a very high voltage driving a low current can minimize the heat lost.

The high-tension ("tension" here just means voltage) lines fan out from

Transformers at substations or on high-voltage lines (as here) step the voltage of the power supply down for use in homes.

the plant in all directions to cities and towns in the area that it serves.

These voltages are extremely dangerous, and the wires must be carried on tall towers (pylons) well off

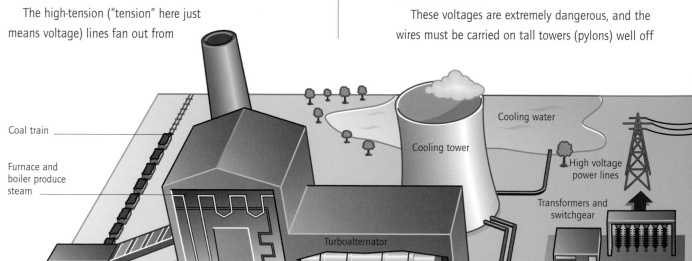

Coal train

Furnace and boiler produce steam

Turboalternator

Cooling water

Cooling tower

Cooling water

High voltage power lines

Transformers and switchgear

Power

SCIENCE WORDS

- **Alternating current (AC):** Electric current that flows first in one direction, then in the other, alternating many times each second. AC is used for domestic electricity supply and many other electrical applications.
- **Direct current (DC):** Electric current that flows in one direction all the time, though it may vary in strength.
- **Insulator:** A material that is a poor conductor of electric current. Examples are rubber, many plastics, and wood. ("Insulator" is also the name given to a poor conductor of heat.)

the ground. They need extra support where they pass over highways. Ceramic insulators keep the current-carrying wires separated from the towers on which they are supported. In some places, high-tension cables are carried in pipes buried underground.

Stepping down

Near an area where there are factories or other industrial plants, power cables lead to an unmanned substation. Here transformers reduce the voltages. A variety of different voltages are produced to meet the needs of different users. The substation runs automatically. It is securely fenced off because it is extremely dangerous for any unauthorized person to wander into it.

Where power is to be delivered to homes, the voltage is finally reduced to about 110 volts (in the United States; about 240 volts in some other countries). The power is brought to an individual home along an overhead cable or under the street.

AC and DC generators

When a coil of wire rotates in a magnetic field the current in it is automatically AC. Think about what happens on one side of a single coil: the current in it alternately flows along it one way and then the opposite way because that side of the coil moves through the magnetic field one

A power plant converts the stored energy of its fuel into steam, which a turboalternator uses to produce a supply of electric current at tens of thousands of volts. A high proportion of the fuel's energy is inevitably lost as waste heat. Transformers boost the voltage for long-distance transmission. At substations, the voltage is stepped down to supply industry and stepped down still further to supply homes and offices.

Industry

City

Substation

Town

Substation

PRINCIPLE OF AC AND DC GENERATORS

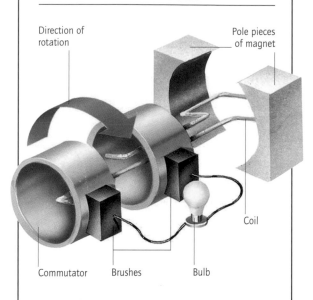

Direction of rotation

Pole pieces of magnet

Coil

Commutator   Brushes   Bulb

In an AC generator each side of the coil is always in contact with the same terminal so that an AC current is delivered.

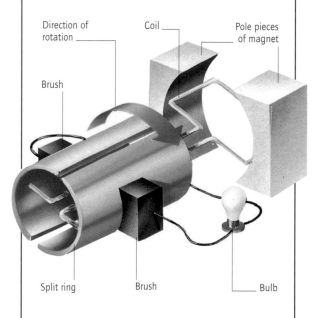

Direction of rotation

Coil

Pole pieces of magnet

Brush

Split ring   Brush   Bulb

In this simplified DC generator split-ring commutators convert the AC voltage from the rotating coil into a DC current.

way in one half of its revolution and the other way in the other half. AC current can then be drawn from the coil by having a terminal of the external circuit that is permanently connected to each side of the coil (see the top illustration in the box feature left for the principle).

Sometimes it is advantageous to produce DC current. In this case, the connections to the generator have to be more complicated. The two terminals of the rotating coil can be in the form of the two halves of a split ring. They make contact alternately with one terminal of the external circuit and then the other (see the bottom illustration in the box feature left). This reverses the connection at the moment the voltage in the rotating coil reverses. The current in the external circuit is DC, though it changes in strength during each rotation of the coil.

Practical generators have to be much more complicated than this. There is a set of rotating coils, and current is drawn only from the coil that is experiencing a peak voltage at that moment. The magnetic field is provided by an electromagnet— that is, it is generated by electric current flowing in special coils.

A pressurized water reactor (PWR) at the South Ukraine nuclear power plant. PWRs work on the fission principle.

Nuclear power

Electricity can also be generated from the energy released by nuclear fission or fusion. There are various designs of nuclear reactor, which differ mainly in the coolant they use. One of the greatest problems facing the designer of a practical nuclear power plant is the radioactivity of the reactor. Neutrons from the fission processes penetrate thick layers of most materials. To shield the outside world from these neutrons, there is always a protective shield, called a biological shield, surrounding the reactor. But the coolant—the fluid that flows through the reactor and takes away its heat to be used—becomes intensely radioactive.

GENERATING ELECTRICITY FROM NUCLEAR ENERGY

Just as in coal- or oil-fired power stations, nuclear power stations use the heat they generate to produce steam, which drives turbines. The turbines in turn drive electrical generators.

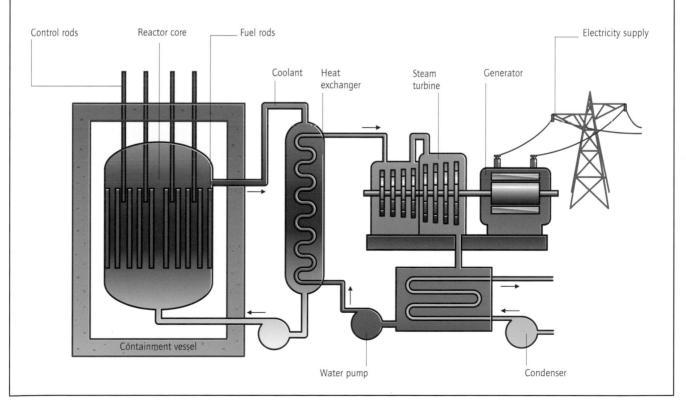

SCIENCE WORDS

- **Fission:** The splitting of a heavy atomic nucleus into two roughly equal parts, with the release of energy.
- **Neutron:** An elementary particle that is electrically neutral (uncharged) and has approximately the same mass as the proton. Outside the nucleus it decays into a proton, an electron, and an antineutrino (the antiparticle of a neutrino).
- **Reactor:** A device for generating energy, either by nuclear fission or by nuclear fusion.

In boiling-water reactors (BWRs)—a type of pressurized water reactor—ordinary water is used as the coolant. It boils in the reactor, and the steam drives turbines directly. In other types of reactor, the coolant flows in a closed circuit and so makes no direct contact with the outside world. It is led around other pipes carrying water, which is heated to boiling point. The steam from the boiling water drives turbines. Each turbine consists of a series of wheels carrying blades. As the hot steam flows through the turbine, it forces the wheels to spin, driving an electricity generator.

After passing through the turbines, the steam is still hot and at quite a high pressure. It then needs to be condensed—turned back into water—to go around the circuit and be boiled again. So it is cooled by being passed over other pipes carrying cold water from some external source such as a nearby river or lake.

Alternative energy sources

Many people are concerned about our use of fossil fuels—coal, oil, and gas—because mining and burning them pollutes the environment, and because there are only limited reserves of them. They fear nuclear energy even more because of the problem of disposing of radioactive waste and the possibility of a serious accident that would release poisonous radioactivity into the atmosphere. They look to sunlight, the wind, waves, tides, and geothermal energy as clean and unlimited alternatives.

Large clusters of wind turbines are a common sight in the windy, low-lying regions of the Netherlands, Denmark, and other northern European countries, and there are also many in California. The electricity is generated in the wind turbine itself. A large machine in favorable conditions can generate around 400 kW. A very large "wind farm" generates as much power as a conventional power plant. But output is very variable, since it depends on weather conditions.

Wave-power machines extract energy from the bobbing motion of sea waves. They are located over a mile (about 2 km) off the coast. The waves' motion may be used to pump air into reservoirs from which it can be released gradually to drive generators. Or it

may be used to rock mechanical devices whose nodding motion is converted into electrical energy. Wave machines are unobtrusive and ideal for use wherever waves are consistently strong.

Solar energy can be turned into electricity in two ways. A large field of mirrors can be used to reflect sunlight onto a boiler, producing steam that drives a turbine in the ordinary way. Large installations in the Mojave Desert use thousands of mirrors to focus sunlight onto a vessel containing a molten salt. The salt's stored heat is used to boil water and make high-pressure steam.

The other method of converting sunlight to electricity is to allow it to shine onto a photoelectric material, which directly generates a current. Photoelectric (or photovoltaic) cells are frequently made from semiconducting materials such as silicon. On a

This solar power plant in the far west of Spain has an output of 50 mW (megawatts), enough to supply electricity to around 25,000 homes. It uses panels of photovoltaic cells to generate current.

small scale such photoelectric cells are used in solar-powered devices such as calculators. Photocells convert about 15 percent of the sunlight's energy into electrical energy. They produce DC current, which has to be converted into AC for large-scale use.

In some US states, the electricity supply is deregulated. Consumers choose an energy company to supply them, and that company accordingly generates more electricity. The difference to the consumer is in the prices that the companies charge and also in the methods of generation they use. Some companies supply "green" electricity generated from "renewable" sources such as hydroelectricity, wind power, or solar energy, and consumers can express their preference for such sources by buying their electricity from those companies.

The blades of wind turbines are shaped as carefully as the propeller or wings of an airplane to extract maximum energy from the wind. A gearbox ensures the generator is driven at the optimal speed.

ELECTRIC VEHICLES

Noise and atmospheric pollution, the bane of modern city life, are caused mostly by motor vehicles. For decades visionaries have dreamed of silent, clean electric cars and trucks. Many companies are working to develop electric vehicles in which the clean, quiet forces of electromagnetism will be put to work to move both people and freight.

A few types of battery-operated vehicle, such as forklift trucks in factories, are used today. In the future, there may be commuter vehicles that get their power wholly from batteries. They would be recharged overnight or perhaps changed when low at the equivalent of a filling station. All present-day batteries are heavy and store relatively little energy. A battery-operated car of today is able to travel only about 90 miles (150 km) before it needs to be recharged.

But in the future, the battery may be combined with, or even replaced by, other devices already in operation experimentally. Ultrafast flywheels could be teamed with batteries. The flywheels would provide bursts of power when needed for acceleration; the batteries would provide steady low power for cruising. The flywheels would have to be made of supertough materials because they would spin at 100,000 revolutions per second, which would tear apart flywheels made from ordinary materials. To reduce friction so that the flywheel did not lose energy, it would be supported on magnetic bearings, held away from physical contact with its container by magnetic fields. The flywheel would need to be revved up from time to time to replace the energy used on journeys.

Energy could also be stored in "ultracapacitors," devices that store large quantities of electricity. Again, they would most likely be teamed with batteries in hybrid systems. There could also be hybrid systems in

which energy-storage devices are combined with gasoline engines to drive electric motors. The gas engine would have to provide only the relatively low power needed for steady cruising. Such an engine would be far more economical and clean than the more powerful engine that is usual in today's vehicles.

Regenerative braking

A feature of all electrical propulsion systems is that some of the energy that is normally wasted in

To try and ease traffic congestion, many cities around the world have invested in light-rail transit systems, with trains powered by electricity from overhead lines. Pictured here is the METRO light-rail system, which began operating in Phoenix, Arizona in 2008.

Electric streetcars

There are many vehicles in the world today that use electrical energy, not from self-contained sources on the vehicle but from the public supply, via rails and overhead lines. Streetcars supplied from overhead electrical lines were popular in many cities in the early 20th century and today are enjoying a revival. They do not have the freedom of movement of gasoline-fueled buses, but are cheaper to run and less polluting.

Electric trains

The major use for electrical vehicle propulsion today is for railroads. Although the first subway trains, in the late 19th century, were steam-powered, electricity was adopted as soon as it became available because steam and smoke were unpleasant and even dangerous in the confines of subway tunnels. Electricity is nearly always preferred for the light railways or rapid-transit systems

braking can be stored and reused. Instead of conventional brakes, magnets attached to a vehicle's wheels induce electric currents in a circuit and charge up a battery, or store the energy some other way, while at the same time the vehicle is slowed. Later the stored energy can be used to boost the vehicle's speed.

SCIENCE WORDS

- **Battery:** Two or more electric cells that generate or store electricity.
- **Fuel cell:** A type of electric cell (battery) in which a fuel (such as hydrogen) is converted directly into electricity.
- **Maglev:** Abbreviation for "magnetic levitation", the technology for keeping vehicles such as trains a few inches above the track on which they run by means of mutually repelling magnetic fields, to overcome friction.
- **Superconductivity:** The property of conducting electricity with no resistance at all. Some metals do this when cooled to a temperature close to absolute zero (−459.67°F/−273.15°C). New complex substances have been developed that superconduct at ever higher temperatures (though not yet as high as 32°F/0°C).

being built in increasing numbers of cities. And it is also the preferred system of powering long-distance trains all over Europe. However, even diesel trains are usually better described as diesel-electric, because most use their diesel engines to generate the electricity that turns the wheels.

Since 1981, France has had a network of high-speed rail services operated by electric trains called TGVs (an abbreviation of *Train à Grande Vitesse*—High-Speed Train). Each train is propelled by two power cars, one at each end. One of them collects power from overhead lines by an assembly called a pantograph—different ones for lower- and higher-voltage supplies. Part of the power is sent along cables to the other power car. Each motor delivers 1,100 kilowatts. The latest TGVs operate at 225 mph (360 km/h), and in the future they may exceed 250 mph (400 km/h) in normal service.

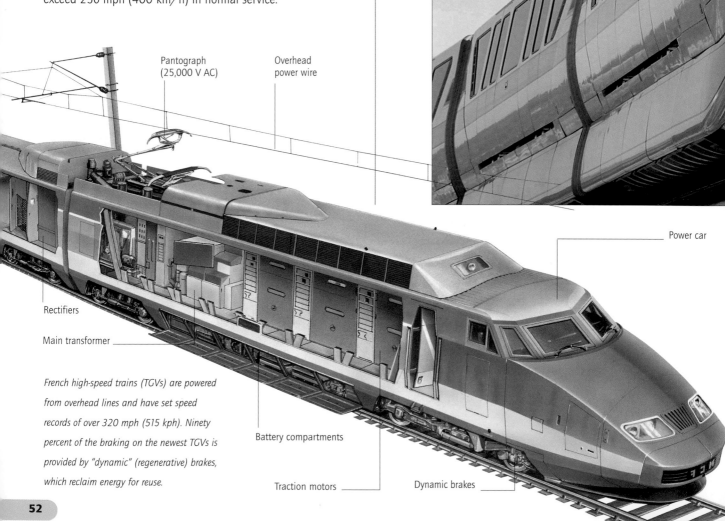

Pantograph
(25,000 V AC)

Overhead
power wire

Power car

Rectifiers

Main transformer

French high-speed trains (TGVs) are powered from overhead lines and have set speed records of over 320 mph (515 kph). Ninety percent of the braking on the newest TGVs is provided by "dynamic" (regenerative) brakes, which reclaim energy for reuse.

Battery compartments

Traction motors

Dynamic brakes

Maglev trains

Still faster speeds will become a reality if trains are separated from the track altogether. That can be done by setting up powerful magnetic fields in the body of the train and in the track that repel each other, a process called magnetic levitation, or maglev. Maglev trains can be supported by repulsion, with the whole train and its magnets above the track, or by attraction, with "wings" mounted on the bottom of the train to carry its magnets. They curl around under the track and are lifted up toward it. Germany has so far been the world leader in maglev technology, developing the Transrapid system, which it has exported to China.

A maglev train on its elevated track. The first (and so far only) commercial maglev entered service in China in 2002, linking the city of Shanghai with Pudong International Airport.

Maglev trains are economical because there is almost no resistance between the train and the track. Also, if they use superconducting magnets, in which the magnet has been cooled to such a temperature that it has no electrical resistance, then very little energy is lost in maintaining the field. Superconducting maglev trains could become the most advanced way of harnessing magnetism to meet the world's future transport needs.

MAGLEV PROPULSION

Powerful superconducting magnets in the body of the train keep it suspended and centered over the track by repulsion from the traveling magnetic poles in the trackbed and at the sides of the track.

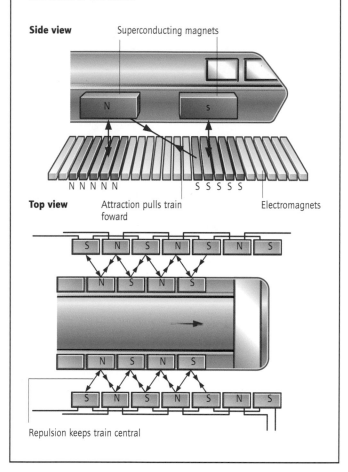

Side view

Superconducting magnets

N   S

N N N N   S S S S

Top view   Attraction pulls train foward

Electromagnets

Repulsion keeps train central

Electric cars

Scientists and engineers everywhere are working hard to exploit the potential of photoelectric cells. These cells are already indispensable in spacecraft, which can be powered for many years by sunlight, which in space is uninterrupted and undimmed by Earth's hazy or cloudy atmosphere.

Experimental vehicles have been developed that run on solar energy alone. Many of them compete in an annual race from north to south across Australia. Winners have reached speeds of 50 mph (80 km/h),

but this is under exceptionally favorable conditions and with machines that are swathed in solar cells and highly streamlined.

Practical electric cars are already at an advanced stage of development. They use batteries rather than solar energy. As batteries that are more compact, lighter, and capable of storing more energy come on the market, electric cars will begin to rival gasoline-driven cars for city use. When the car's batteries are nearly run down, the driver goes to a resupply point—perhaps at an ordinary gas station—and exchanges the old batteries for new, freshly charged ones.

Another radical innovation in motive power is the fuel cell, an alternative to the battery. It generates electricity from chemical reactions, as do batteries, but with the difference that the chemicals are supplied continuously from outside. Many types have been developed, using a variety of fuels, including hydrogen, methane, and carbon monoxide, reacting with air. Often the only waste product is water.

With growing concerns about carbon emissions and global warming, automobile manufacturers are busy developing alternatives to the internal combustion engine, such as this "hybrid" car (right), which runs alternately on gasoline and electricity.

SCIENCE WORDS

- ***n*-type semiconductor:** A semiconductor material in which current consists mostly of electrons in motion.
- ***p*-type semiconductor:** A semiconductor material in which current consists mostly of moving holes.
- **Photoelectric cell (photocell):** A device that uses light or other electromagnetic radiation to produce a current or voltage. Photocells are commonly used in photographic exposure meters and burglar alarms.

SOLAR POWER

This solar-powered vehicle (seen from above), covered in photoelectric cells, traveled in the bright sunshine of the Australian deserts at an average speed of 30 mph (50 km/h). It took part in the annual race for such vehicles, run from Darwin to Adelaide.

Each solar cell consists of layers of two types of semiconductor, called p-type and n-type, sandwiched between metal films.

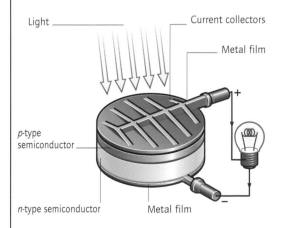

Light — Current collectors

Metal film

p-type semiconductor

n-type semiconductor — Metal film

BATTERIES

On the preceding pages, we saw how the new generation of electric and "hybrid" cars will be powered by batteries and fuel cells. We will now look at the history of these devices, and examine how different types of cell generate electricity.

Batteries are a way of converting chemical energy into electrical energy. There are two main kinds, known as a primary cell and a secondary cell. In a primary cell, the chemicals it contains are gradually used up. When they have been consumed, the battery no longer produces electric current.

A secondary cell is similar except that when the chemicals have been used up, the battery can be recharged. By pushing an electric current through the cell (rather as in electrolysis), the chemicals are regenerated, and the battery will work again. Because a secondary cell effectively stores or accumulates the charge put into it, this type of battery is also called an accumulator. An accumulator can be discharged and recharged over and over again.

The first batteries

In around 1800, the Italian physicist Alessandro Volta (1745–1827) made the first battery. It consisted of

SCIENCE WORDS

- **Anode:** An electrode with a positive charge, at which electrons leave a system.
- **Cathode:** An electrode with a negative charge, at which electrons enter a system.
- **Electrolysis:** The decomposition of an electrolyte by electric current, using two electrodes.
- **Polarization:** The process that causes bubbles of gas to appear on one of the electrodes of an electric cell, stopping the cell from working.

alternating disks of copper and zinc, separated by disks of cloth, leather, or paper soaked in salt solution. A length of wire was attached to the topmost copper disk, and another wire was connected to the bottom zinc disk. Because it consisted of a stack of disks, the battery came to be known as the "voltaic pile."

The pile works by electrochemical processes. The copper metal loses electrons to the solution between the disks and forms copper ions. At the same time, zinc dissolves in the solution and releases hydrogen gas. If the wires are joined in an electric circuit, current flows

Alessandro Volta became internationally famous after he invented the voltaic pile in about 1800. Here he is (left) demonstrating it to the French Emperor Napoleon.

from the positive copper disk through the circuit and into the negative zinc disk. The disks are simply electrodes.

The next stage in the development of the battery was a simple cell made by immersing a copper plate (anode) and a zinc plate (cathode) in a solution of dilute sulfuric acid. When a length of wire connects the plates, current flows from the copper to the zinc.

Alessandro Volta

Volta's full name was Count Alessandro Giuseppe Antonio Anastasio Volta. He was born in 1745 in Como, Italy. Unlike his male relatives, who nearly all became priests, Volta decided to study electricity. In 1774, he invented the electrophorus, a device that could produce and store a static electric charge. But his best known invention was the first battery to produce a steady electric current. This consisted of a pile of alternating disks of copper and zinc separated by pieces of cloth soaked in salt solution. It became known as the voltaic pile. Volta died in 1827, some years before the unit of potential difference was named the volt to honor his achievement.

FIRST BATTERY

Because the first battery consisted of a stack of disks, it was christened a pile. It was called a voltaic pile after Alessandro Volta, the Italian scientist who made the first one. It had alternate disks of copper and zinc separated by disks of cloth soaked in salt solution.

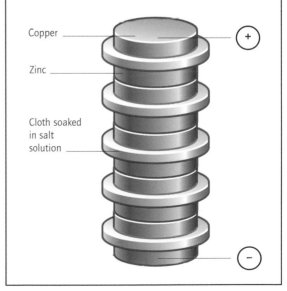

Copper ——————————— (+)

Zinc ————

Cloth soaked in salt solution ————

(−)

Negative sulfate ions from the acid electrolyte travel to the zinc electrode, where the zinc dissolves to form zinc ions. At the same time, positive hydrogen ions travel to the copper electrode, where they are discharged to produce bubbles of hydrogen gas. As soon as hydrogen bubbles cover the copper electrode, the action of the cells slows down and eventually stops. When this happens, the cell is said to be polarized.

Practical batteries

The first attempt to find a way around the problem of polarization was made by a British physicist named John Daniell (1790–1845). In the so-called Daniell cell, the copper electrode (anode) takes the form of a cylindrical copper container. The zinc electrode (cathode) is a metal rod inside a porous earthenware pot containing dilute sulfuric acid. The porous pot stands inside the copper container, and between the two there is a solution of copper sulfate.

Lead–acid car batteries for scrap. Almost all the lead can be reclaimed. To encourage recycling, many U.S. states charge a deposit on new batteries, which is refunded when the exhausted battery is returned.

When a length of wire connects the electrodes, hydrogen ions travel toward the inside of the copper container. But because of the presence of the copper sulfate solution, instead of hydrogen gas being released, copper metal is deposited on the container. There is no polarization, and in this cell the copper sulfate acts as a depolarizer. At the zinc electrode, zinc sulfate is again formed as in the simple cell. A Daniell cell produces about 1.1 volts.

A different depolarizer is used in a cell invented in 1865 by the French scientist Georges Leclanché

DRY BATTERY

A dry battery as used in a flashlight is a type of Leclanché cell that has a paste of ammonium chloride as the electrolyte.

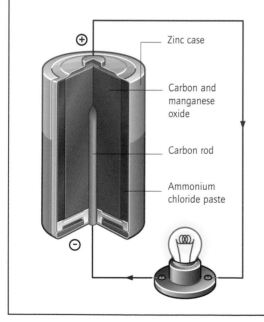

- ⊕
- Zinc case
- Carbon and manganese oxide
- Carbon rod
- Ammonium chloride paste
- ⊖

THE DANIELL CELL

The Daniell cell is a type of voltaic invented by John Daniell (1790-1845). The anode is solid copper and the cathode is zinc metal. The cell has two electrolytes. The anode is in copper sulfate solution, while the cathode is in sulfuric acid. The two liquids are separated by a porous barrier. The zinc atoms in the cathode are oxidized. They lose two electrons and form zinc ions (Zn^{2+}). These ions dissolve in the acid. The copper ions (Cu^{2+}) in the copper sulfate are reduced. They pick up electrons from the anode and form copper atoms, which join on to the anode. The electrons released in the cathode move through a wire to the anode, producing an electric current of 1 volt.

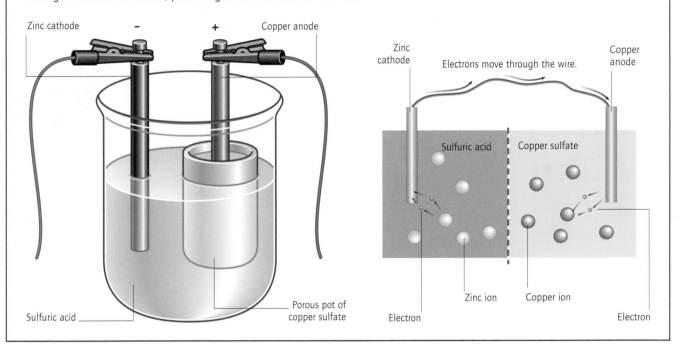

(1839-1882). In the Leclanché cell, a zinc cathode dips into a container of ammonium chloride solution. The anode is a carbon rod surrounded by a depolarizer of manganese dioxide. Powdered carbon is mixed with the manganese dioxide to make it a better conductor. Hydrogen is still produced at the anode, but the manganese dioxide gets rid of it by converting it to water. A Leclanché cell produces about 1.5 volts. To get a higher voltage, several cells are joined in a group, or battery—which is why primary cells are called batteries.

Away with water

The cells described so far are all wet cells—they have various solutions as their electrolytes. This does not make the batteries very portable. The problem is overcome in a dry battery, which contains no liquid. It is a type of Leclanché cell, but the electrolyte is a paste of ammonium chloride and gum. The zinc cathode forms the case of the battery, and manganese dioxide and carbon again surround the central carbon anode. Dry cells of this kind are commonly used in flashlights and portable radios.

There are many other types of dry battery, including the mercury oxide cell, which is used in many electronic watches. It produces 1.35 volts. A Leclanché-type cell with zinc chloride instead of ammonium chloride works better at lower temperatures. A nickel-cadmium cell is different because it can be recharged after it has run down by connecting it to an external supply of current. It is therefore a type of secondary cell, or accumulator.

LEAD–ACID ACCUMULATOR

A common accumulator has electrodes of lead and lead oxide in an electrolyte of sulfuric acid. It produces about 2 volts. A car battery has six lead–acid cells, giving a total voltage of 12 volts. When the battery has run down, connecting it to an outside source of current recharges it.

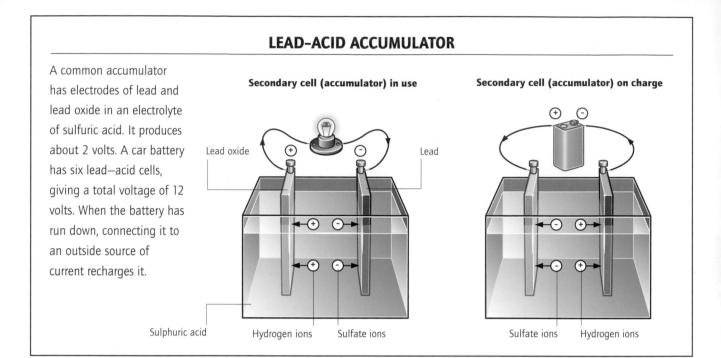

Secondary cell (accumulator) in use

Lead oxide · Lead

Sulphuric acid · Hydrogen ions · Sulfate ions

Secondary cell (accumulator) on charge

Sulfate ions · Hydrogen ions

Accumulators

The best-known type of accumulator is a car battery, used as the basic source of electricity in an automobile.

Thomas Alva Edison

Edison was one of the greatest inventors of his age. By the time he died in 1931, he had more than 1,300 patents to his name. He was born in Milan, Ohio, in 1847 and was taught at home by his mother—he did not do well at school because of deafness. He moved to Port Huron, Michigan, in 1854, and as a teenager he used to sell newspapers on the railroad there. He grew interested in the telegraph and was soon inventing his own equipment. Edison set up a laboratory at Menlo Park, New Jersey, where he made some of his best known inventions, including the phonograph and the electric light bulb. He was the first to see the allure of electric power and opened the world's first electric power plant in New York in 1882. Ten years later, Edison's various companies merged to form the General Electric Company (GEC).

The usual kind has cathodes made of lead and anodes made of lead covered with a layer of lead oxide. The electrolyte is sulfuric acid. When the accumulator is in use, sulfate ions react with the lead cathode to produce lead sulfate and release electrons. At the anode, hydrogen ions (from the acid) and sulfate ions react with the lead oxide to produce lead sulfate and water. This reaction needs a supply of electrons.

To recharge the accumulator, current from an outside source is passed through the battery in the opposite direction. This has the effect of reversing the reactions at the electrodes, re-forming lead and lead oxide. The accumulator is then ready for use again.

In an automobile, the battery is used mainly to start the motor. Once the motor is running, an alternator supplies current to recharge the battery. A lead-acid cell produces about 2 volts. A car battery has six cells, giving a total voltage of 12 volts.

There are several other kinds of accumulator. One is the nickel-iron accumulator, invented by Thomas Alva Edison (1847-1931) and known also as a NIFE cell (after the chemical symbols for nickel, Ni, and iron, Fe). The electrolyte is potassium hydroxide.

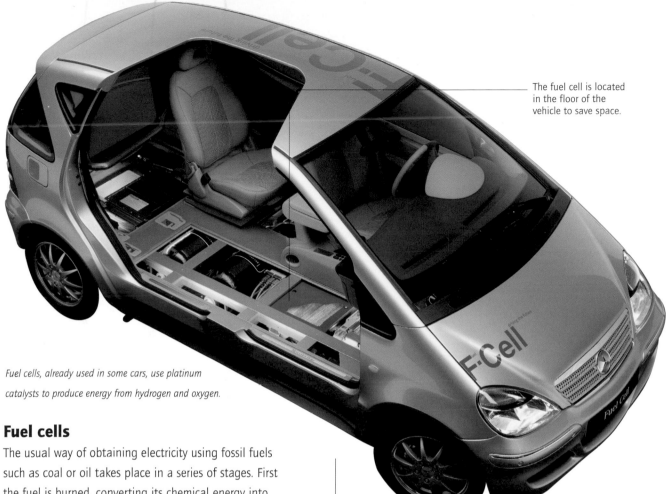

The fuel cell is located in the floor of the vehicle to save space.

Fuel cells, already used in some cars, use platinum catalysts to produce energy from hydrogen and oxygen.

Fuel cells

The usual way of obtaining electricity using fossil fuels such as coal or oil takes place in a series of stages. First the fuel is burned, converting its chemical energy into heat. The heat boils water in a boiler to produce steam. The steam then turns a turbine, which finally rotates a generator to produce electricity. There are energy losses at each stage, making the whole process very inefficient. A fuel cell is a type of battery in which a fuel is converted directly into electricity. It never runs down, as a dry battery does, and it never needs recharging, as an accumulator does.

One type of fuel cell uses hydrogen gas as fuel and also requires a supply of oxygen. The electrolyte is potassium hydroxide solution. Hydrogen is pumped into a hollow, porous cathode where it reacts with hydroxyl ions to produce water and a supply of electrons. At the hollow anode, oxygen reacts with water to produce a new supply of hydroxyl ions. The overall reaction is the chemical combination of hydrogen and oxygen to form water, with the generation of electricity.

SCIENCE WORDS

- **Electrode:** A metal plate or carbon rod that carries electrons into or out of a battery (cell), electrolysis cell, or vacuum tube.
- **Electrolyte:** A liquid that conducts electricity, as in a battery or in electrolysis.
- **Primary cell:** A type of electric cell in which chemical reactions produce electricity. When the chemicals are used up, the cell is discharged and cannot be recharged.
- **Secondary cell:** A type of electric cell in which chemical reactions produce electricity. Unlike a primary cell, it can be recharged.

GLOSSARY

AC motor An electric motor that is operated by alternating current.

Alternating current (AC) Electric current that flows first in one direction, then in the other, alternating many times each second.

Anode An electrode with a positive charge, at which electrons leave a system.

Bar magnet A bar-shaped permanent magnet, with a magnetic pole at each end.

Cathode An electrode with a negative charge, at which electrons enter a system.

Coil A spiral of wire through which an electric current flows.

Current A flow of electric charge (electrons). Current may be supplied by the domestic electricity supply, generators, or batteries.

DC motor An electric motor that is operated by direct current.

Direct current (DC) Electric current that flows in one direction all the time, though it may vary in strength.

Domain A small region in a magnetic material in which the magnetic fields of individual atoms all point in the same direction, making the domain into a single small magnet.

Electrode A metal plate or carbon rod that carries electrons into or out of a battery (cell), electrolysis cell, or vacuum tube.

Electrolysis The decomposition of an electrolyte by electric current, using two electrodes.

Electrolyte A liquid that conducts electricity, as in a battery or in electrolysis.

Electromagnet A device that develops a magnetic field when electric current is passed through it. It consists of a coil with a core.

Electromagnetism The interlinked phenomena of electricity and magnetism. Every electric current generates a magnetic field, while changes in a magnetic field can cause a current to flow.

Electromotive force (e.m.f.) An electrical influence that tends to cause electric current to flow. E.m.f. is exerted by batteries and electric generators.

Field The pattern of magnetic, electric, gravitational, or other influence around an object.

Fission The splitting of a heavy atomic nucleus into two roughly equal parts, with the release of energy.

Fuel cell A type of electric cell (battery) in which a fuel (such as hydrogen) is converted directly into electricity.

Induction motor An electric motor in which a moving magnetic field induces (generates) current in another component, which moves to follow the field. The moving part may revolve or move in a straight line.

Insulator A material that is a poor conductor of electric current.

Line of force An imaginary line whose direction at any point in a field shows the direction of the field at that point.

Linear induction motor An induction motor that produces straight-line motion, as, for example, in making a sliding door close and open.

Lodestone A naturally magnetic iron ore, formerly used to make magnetic compasses.

Magnetic compass A device in which a freely rotating magnetized needle indicates the direction of magnetic north.

Magnetic equator The imaginary circle around the Earth, approximately halfway between the planet's magnetic poles, where the Earth's magnetic field is horizontal.

Magnetic lens An arrangement of electromagnets that can focus a beam of electrons or other charged particles, as in an electron microscope.

Magnetic north The direction in which a magnetic compass points (in the northern hemisphere).

Magnetic resonance imaging (MRI) The technique of making pictures of the inside of something, for example, the living human body.

Magnetization The process of making an object or material into a magnet.

Magnetosphere The region around the Earth or other celestial body, such as Jupiter, in which its magnetic field is stronger than the field in surrounding space.

Motor A machine that converts energy, usually electrical energy, into motion.

Neutron An elementary particle that is electrically neutral (uncharged) and has approximately the same mass as the proton.

Outside the nucleus it decays into a proton, an electron, and an antineutrino (the antiparticle of a neutrino).

n-type semiconductor A semiconductor material in which current consists mostly of electrons in motion.

Photoelectric cell (photocell) A device that uses light or other electromagnetic radiation to produce a current or voltage.

Polarization The process that causes bubbles of gas to appear on one of the electrodes of an electric cell, stopping the cell from working.

Pole One of the two regions of a magnet where the strength of the field is greatest. Lines of force diverge (radiate out) from one pole and converge on the other.

Primary cell A type of electric cell in which chemical reactions produce electricity. When the chemicals are used up, the cell is discharged and cannot be recharged.

p-type semiconductor A semiconductor material in which current consists mostly of moving holes.

Relay A device that is activated by changes in an electric current in a circuit, causing it to switch a second electric circuit on or off. Relays often incorporate electromagnets.

Rotor In electromagnetic technology, the rotating coil in a motor or generator.

Secondary cell A type of electric cell in which chemical reactions produce electricity. Unlike a primary cell, it can be recharged.

Solenoid A current-carrying coil of wire.

Stator The stationary part of a motor or generator.

Superconductivity The property of conducting electricity in which there is no resistance at all.

Torque Any force or system of forces that cause rotation.

Transformer A device that increases or decreases the voltage of alternating current.

Turbine A machine in which the energy of a moving fluid or air flow is converted into mechanical energy by causing a bladed rotor to rotate.

Van Allen belts Another name for the Earth's radiation belts.

FURTHER RESEARCH

Books – General

Bloomfield, Louis A. *How Things Work: The Physics of Everyday Life.* Hoboken, NJ: Wiley, 2009.

Bloomfield, Louis A. *How Everything Works: Making Physics Out of the Ordinary.* Hoboken, NJ: Wiley, 2007.

Daintith, John. *A Dictionary of Physics.* New York, NY: Oxford University Press, 2010.

De Pree, Christopher. *Physics Made Simple.* New York, NY: Broadway Books, 2005.

Epstein, Lewis Carroll. *Thinking Physics: Understandable Practical Reality.* San Francisco, CA: Insight Press, 2009.

Glencoe McGraw-Hill. *Introduction to Physical Science.* Blacklick, OH: Glencoe/McGraw-Hill, 2007.

Heilbron, John L. *The Oxford Guide to the History of Physics and Astronomy.* New York, NY: Oxford University Press, 2005.

Holzner, Steve. *Physics Essentials For Dummies.* Hoboken, NJ: For Dummies, 2010.

Jargodzk, Christopher, and Potter, Franklin. *Mad About Physics: Braintwisters, Paradoxes, and Curiosities.* Hoboken, NJ: Wiley, 2000.

Lehrman, Robert L. *E-Z Physics.* Hauppauge, NY: Barron's Educational, 2009.

Lloyd, Sarah. *Physics: IGCSE Revision Guide.* New York, NY: Oxford University Press, 2009.

Suplee, Curt. *Physics in the 20th Century.* New York, NY: Harry N. Abrams, 2002.

Taylor, Charles (ed). *The Kingfisher Science Encyclopedia,* Boston, MA: Kingfisher Books, 2006.

Walker, Jearl. *The Flying Circus of Physics.* Hoboken, NJ: Wiley, 2006.

Watts, Lisa et al. *The Most Explosive Science Book in the Universe... by the Brainwaves.* New York, NY: DK Publishing, 2009.

Zitzewitz, Paul W. *Physics Principles and Problems.* Columbus, OH: McGraw-Hill, 2005.

Books – Magnetism

Barnett, Dave, and Bjornsgaard, Kirk. *Electric Power Generation: A Nontechnical Guide.* Tulsa, OK: Pennwell Books, 2000.

Cheshire, Gerard. *Electricity & Magnetism (Fundamental Physics).* Mankato, MN: Smart Apple Media, 2006.

Coey, Michael. *Magnetism and Magnetic Materials.* New York, NY: Cambridge University Press, 2010.

DiSpezio, Michael Anthony. *Awesome Experiments in Electricity and Magnetism.* New York, NY: Sterling, 2007.

Gardner, Robert. *Electricity and Magnetism Science Fair Projects.* Berkeley Heights, NJ: Enslow Publishers, 2010.

Hughes, Austin. *Electric Motors and Drives: Fundamentals, Types and Applications.* Burlington, MA: Newnes, 2005.

Jeffs, Eric. *Green Energy: Sustainable Electricity Supply with Low Environmental Impact.* Boca Raton, FL: CRC Press, 2009.

Padilla, Michael J. et al. *Science Explorer: Electricity and Magnetism.* Upper Saddle River, NJ: Pearson Prentice Hall, 2006.

School Specialty Publishing. *Magnetism (The Science Search Lab).* Greensboro, NC: School Specialty Publishing, 2005.

Web Sites

Marvellous machines
www.galaxy.net/~k12/machines/index.shtml
Experiments about simple machines.

How Stuff Works – Physical Science
http://science.howstuffworks.com/physical-science-channel.htm
Topics on all aspects of physics.

PhysLink.com
www.physlink.com/SiteInfo/Index.cfm
Physics and astronomy education, research, and reference.

PhysicsCentral
www.physicscentral.com/about/index.cfm
Education site of the American Physical Society.

Physics 2000
www.colorado.edu/physics/2000/index.pl
An interactive journey through modern physics.

The Why Files
http://whyfiles.org/
The science behind the news.